NEVADA MOUNTAIN RANGES

TEXT & PHOTOGRAPHY BY GEORGE WUERTHNER

Nevada
GEOGRAPHIC SERIES
NUMBER 1

AMERICAN & WORLD GEOGRAPHIC PUBLISHING

DEDICATION

This book is dedicated to the men and women who love Nevada and its mountains. Many have labored for decades trying to develop a new ethic towards Nevada's landscape, and in particular an appreciation for wilderness values. The Friends of Nevada Wilderness and the Toiyabe chapter of the Sierra Club deserve special mention for their hard work over the years.

ACKNOWLEDGMENTS

I had a lot of help from many individuals from various Nevada state offices, the Nature Conservancy, U.S. Forest Service, Bureau of Land Management, National Park Service, Chambers of Commerce, and from museum curators and librarians at the University of Nevada, Reno and in Elko. In addition, a number of individuals gave me personal attention of suggestions that were particularly valuable, and they include: Jan Roberts, Rose Strickland, Charlie Watson, Dan Heitz, Jan Nachlinger, Glenn Glemmer, Jim Morefield, Roger Rosentreter, Al Hendricks, Marjorie Sills, David Lambert, Barry Reiswig, and Alvin McLane, author of *Silent Cordilleras*.

Library of Congress Cataloging-in-Publication

Wuerthner, George.
 Nevada mountain ranges / text & photography by George Wuerthner
   p.   cm. -- (Nevada geographic series : no. 1)
   Includes index.
   ISBN 1-56037-014-9
   1. Mountains--Nevada. 2. Nevada-- Geography. I. Title. II. Series.
F845.W84 1992
917.9302--dc20   92-5795

Text and photography © 1992 George Wuerthner
© 1992 American & World Geographic Publishing
P.O. Box 5630, Helena, MT 59604
Printed in Hong Kong by Nordica International Ltd

CONTENTS

Left: Frémont Culture pictographs in Baker Creek Canyon of Great Basin National Park. JEFF GNASS PHOTO
Facing page, top: Junipers and pinyon pines above Spring Valley in the Snake Range. JEFF GNASS PHOTO
Bottom: Lush growth in ungrazed segment of Upper Mary's River, Jarbidge Wilderness, Humboldt National Forest.
Title page: At Sacramento Pass in the Snake Range.

Front cover: Wind-sculpted limber pines cling to a talus slope on the north ridge of Wheeler Peak, Great Basin National Park. JEFF GNASS PHOTO
Back cover, top: In the Ruby Mountains. LARRY PROSOR PHOTO
Bottom: Autumn aspen in Lamoille Canyon. JEFF GNASS PHOTO

INTRODUCTION

Most people driving across Nevada on I-80 or I-15 barely stop for more than a quick tank of gas. At most they may spend some time slipping quarters into the slot machines that greet them at nearly every border crossing, or wandering into the neon gaming rooms of Reno or Las Vegas. To the average visitor or to the traveler trying to reach the Pacific or Rockies, Nevada seems like a wasteland, a place that *should* be the nation's nuclear waste dump. Many adjectives come to mind. Dry. Remote. Desolate. Barren. Empty. Boring. Step on the gas, hold it at 75 mph and hope it will end soon.

In many respects such descriptions are at least partially right. It is dry. Remote. And wonderfully empty. But for those with an appreciative eye, it is anything but boring—especially if you like mountains. This book is meant to be an introduction to all those "empty, boring" places in between rest areas and slot machines.

Nevada is, upon closer examination, a poor person's Alaska. It has some of the wildest, most remote, least-traveled country this side of Canada and, unlike Alaska, it won't cost you a small fortune to visit and explore. Drive off the four-lane, take some time to go up a dirt road that peters out on some mountainside. Get out of your vehicle and head into the hills on foot to really appreciate Nevada—to know the feel of the noon sun beating down on you and the cool of the evening twilight, to hear the rustle of aspen or smell the scent of sagebrush after a thunderstorm.

Nevada Mountains

The name Nevada means "snow-capped" in Spanish and, indeed, there is no shortage of snow-capped peaks in this state. In an area that runs 484 miles from north to south and 320 miles east to west, more mountain ranges can be found than in any other state in the nation—at least 160 major named mountain masses, plus another hundred hills, individual peaks and uplands. Alvin McLane, author of *Silent Cordilleras* and one of the leading authorities on Nevada mountains, lists 314 individual ranges and hills, although not all have official names.

The average elevation of Nevada is above 5,000 feet. From a low of 470 feet near Laughlin on the Colorado River to 13,140 feet on the summit of the state's highest eminence—Boundary Peak in the White Mountains on the California border—Nevada has one of the greatest spans of relief of any state in the nation.

In addition to the White Mountains, Nevada has eight other ranges with one or more peaks exceeding 11,000 feet, including the Snake Range, Schell Creek Range, Grant Range, White Pine Range, Toiyabe Range, Toquima Range, Wassuk Mountains and the Spring Mountains. The Spring Mountains near Las Vegas are probably the most dramatic mountain range in Nevada, leaping nearly 10,000 feet into the desert sky. From their base near 2,000 feet to the alpine summit of Charleston Peak at 11,912 feet, the Spring Mountains have one of the steepest vertical reliefs found in the United States. Dozens of other Nevada ranges have peaks exceeding 10,000 feet.

If you have ever driven across the state on Highway 50 or one of the other east-west roads that cross Nevada between Utah and California, the sensation of being on a roller coaster is hard to dismiss. You climb a mountain range, slide down the other side, cross a long, wide valley, then begin to ascend again. There is a cadence: Snake Range, Spring Valley; Schell Creek Range, Steptoe Valley; Egan Range, Jakes Valley; White Pine Range, Newark Valley. Basin and range. Parallel mountain chains defined by northeast-southwest faults, with row upon row of long, linear ranges, most between 50 and 100 miles in length, seemingly crawling across the state in a wide procession. In fact, one writer characterized the state's mountains as an army of caterpillars marching northward.

The parallel symmetry of mountain and valley is created by tectonic forces that are slowly stretching Nevada apart. During the last 24 million or so years, the air-mile distance between Utah's Wasatch Range, the eastern edge of the Basin and Range province, and California's Sierra Nevada at the western bounds, has increased by 50 miles. As the earth's crust has been pulled apart, valleys fell along faults and chunks of the crust became ridges and mountains.

Great Basin and Mojave

Basin and range refers to the region's geological makeup, while Great Basin, a name created by explorer John Frémont in 1844, has a biogeographical basis. Fremont noted that in a vast area of the Intermountain West, the rivers run nowhere—that is, they never reach the sea. For instance, Nevada's Humboldt River has its headwaters in northeastern Nevada and drains into Humboldt Sink, a huge playa (part of an even larger ancient lake bed) east of Reno where the waters eventually evaporate. The Great Basin, however, is not a single basin, but dozens of basins with no external drainage—some with lakes and some without.

Great Basin has also come to refer to the cold desert plant community, dominated by sagebrush and bunchgrasses, that is so common across most of Nevada. The Great Basin desert is one of four major desert types found in North America. Dominated by freezing winter temperatures and snow, it receives most precipitation during the winter months. The borders of the Great Basin are not precisely drawn, but it includes nearly five sixths of Nevada and parts of eastern Oregon, California east of the Sierra, southern Idaho, southwestern Wyoming and western Utah. But most of this desert is found in Nevada and one could say that if any part of the West can be considered "quintessential" Great Basin, it is Nevada.

While all of Nevada falls into the Basin and Range province, the entire state is not within the Great Basin geographical-biological region. Southern Nevada, cutting a roughly diagonal line that starts near Caliente on the eastern edge of the state and trends southwest towards Beatty near Death Valley, is part of the Mojave Desert. The Mojave is warmer and lower in elevation. Instead of sagebrush, the landscape is covered sparsely with creosote bush, shadscale, black brush, cactus and Joshua tree.

Within these broad desert classifications, there are some smaller, more discrete Nevada deserts. But keep in mind that almost all of Nevada's valleys can be classified as deserts based on evaporation rates and precipitation, so the specific designation of a desert means the area is comparatively more arid or desolate. Because of the plant life supported here, vegetation ecologists classify the Great Basin as "semi-arid" desert. As comparison, the Sahara is labeled "arid."

In the north lies the Forty Mile Desert, which includes the sinks of the Humboldt and Carson rivers. Today, as we skirt across this same distance in less than an hour on Interstate 80, it's hard to imagine how difficult this region was for the California Trail emigrants to cross. Many considered the traverse of the Forty Mile Desert, with its lack of water, forage and sandy washes, the most difficult part of the entire journey from St. Louis to California.

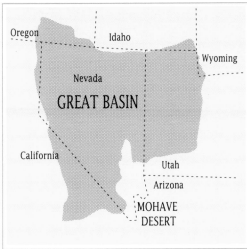

Aspen in fall color below Wheeler Peak.
JEFF GNASS PHOTO

5

To the north of the Forty Mile Desert and Interstate 80 lie the Black Rock and Smoke Creek deserts. The two deserts are actually one and the same, but have different names because a narrow "channel" near Gerlach separates them. The Black Rock/Smoke Creek Desert is really a playa that is periodically re-wetted.

To the south lies the Amargosa Desert, a low valley along the California-Nevada border near Death Valley National Monument. The Amargosa "River" flows out into the desert and disappears.

Disappearing rivers are the norm in Nevada. They simply do not have enough volume to flow to the sea before they evaporate. With the exception of the Colorado, which forms the state's southern border with Arizona, and the Snake River tributaries such as the Owyhee, Bruneau, Jarbidge and Salmon Falls rivers in the northeastern part of the state, all other watercourses eventually flow out into wide valleys and sink out of sight. The largest rivers, such as the Walker, Carson and Truckee, all flow off the Sierra Nevada. Other "major" rivers include the Quinn, which flows into the Black Rock Desert and disappears, the Reese River, a tributary of the Humboldt, and Meadow Valley Wash, which drains into the Colorado River near the Utah state line.

Despite the paucity of water, Nevada has a few very large lakes like Pyramid, Walker and Washoe—all remnants from glacial times—but all are disappearing or, as with Winnemucca and Washoe, are already gone due to excessive water diversions for irrigation.

The importance of water—any water—is understood when one considers that Nevada ranks as the driest state in the Union. A statewide average of only nine inches of precipitation falls annually, and some places get considerably less. Las Vegas, for instance, is the most arid major city in the nation, receiving only three to four inches of precipitation a year. Miami, by comparison, gets 55 inches. (But Miami has the Everglades out its back door and Las Vegas—the Mojave Desert.) Reno is considerably cooler and gets a bit more moisture—about 7.5 inches annually—but no one complains about the humidity here either.

Though almost all of Nevada qualifies as desert, that does not necessarily mean it is hot or even warm all the time. Ely's record low is 43 degrees below zero, and even Las Vegas, far to the south and at a low elevation, occasionally experiences frosts.

But hot or cold, there is very little precipitation due to two factors. Nevada sits east of the Sierran mountain mass in what is known as a "rain shadow." Air masses, moving over the high Sierra Nevada mountains in California, cool, condense and release their moisture. Pacific maritime storms drop their water on the western slope of California's mountains and leave little to soak the region to the east. For example, the west side the Sierran crest near Lake Tahoe gets 60 inches of precipitation annually. A weather station at 9,600 feet elevation on Mt. Rose, one of the most easterly of the Sierran peaks near Lake Tahoe, receives only 30 inches. And the town of Washoe, at the base of the Carson Range and no more than six air miles due east of Mt. Rose, gets a mere five inches.

Winter is about the only time Nevada receives precipitation. During the summer, cold ocean currents off the coast of California keep the air above the ocean cool. Consequently, there is little rising air and movement that can carry moisture-laden air masses inland across the Sierra and into the Silver State. Although a few thundershowers occur as a consequence of hot-air lift, only in the very eastern and southeastern regions of the state do more or less predictable "monsoon" summer showers moderate this general pattern. These air masses invade the southwest United States from the Gulf of Mexico, bringing summer thunderstorms. But it is a long way from the Gulf to Nevada, and few storms actually make it that far.

Population and Economy

To anyone who has driven across Nevada on anything but the Interstate, the state seems empty—devoid of signs of people save the ubiquitous barbed wire fence and the occasional isolated ranch. And indeed, Nevada is sparsely settled, with a population density of about nine people per square mile. Only Wyoming, Montana and Alaska have lower densities.

In demographics, Nevada resembles Alaska, with most of the state's population in a few large cities. In fact, despite all the mythic hoopla about cowboys and miners representing the "real" Nevadan, 80 percent of the state's 1.2 million people live in the urban centers of Las Vegas, Reno and Carson City. Clark County, where Las Vegas sits, is home to 659,830 people—more than half the state's population—and another 242,800 people reside in Washoe County, the majority of them in Reno. And these urban areas are among the fastest growing in the nation. Just in the last eight years Clark County has grown by 30 percent, with almost 200,000 new residents. In the late 1980s an estimated 6,000 people a month were moving to Las Vegas alone, a situation that raises questions about how much growth the area can sustain before it begins to choke with smog and traffic jams.

And while Las Vegas and Reno may boom, populations in the hinterlands mostly have declined. With the exception of a few booms spurred by gold mining in towns like Elko or Winnemucca, most of rural Nevada has seen nothing but decreasing populations since the late 1800s. Some counties in Nevada have only a few thousand residents. Esmeralda County has even fewer—only 1,440 residents spread over 777 square miles, or nearly a section of land per inhabitant! And Nye County, with 16,170 square miles, the largest county in Nevada and third largest county in the nation, has only 11,000 or so residents. By contrast, the entire county of Holland is slightly smaller with 15,892 square miles, but has more than 13 million people.

So what do all the people in Las Vegas and Reno do for work? Not surprisingly, given its night life, casinos, and the 25 million tourists that descend on Nevada annually, tourism and recreation ranks as the leading industry and employer, with 50 percent of the population working in tourist-related and service industry fields. While many of the tourists come to gamble in the casinos, outdoor recreation is also a major drawing card. Among the top outdoor attractions are Lake Tahoe and its ski resorts, Lake Mead for water sports, and Great Basin National Park.

Only when you get out into the hinterlands do mining and ranching take on greater roles, but still they are relatively small portions of the state's overall economic picture. In 1991, out of 640,000 employed residents, only approximately 15,000 workers were employed in mining. Out of all Nevada jobs, agriculture contributed even less—only seven tenths of a percent. Nationally, Nevada ranks 49th in agriculture—only Rhode Island produces less.

In eastern and central Nevada, mining is big business. More than 120 mines operate in Nevada today, most of them for extracting gold by cyanide heap leach operations. Most Nevada mines have an estimated life of six to ten years. Unless new deposits are located or the price of minerals rises high enough to enable mining of lower-quality ore, most towns supported by mining operations will suffer inevitable decline.

Water Shortages

While Nevada continues to grow as if it had no limits, reality may soon bring Nevada's boom to a screeching halt. The problem is not jobs, but water. Until 1971, nearly all of Las Vegas got its water from ground-water pumping. Pumping peaked in 1968 when that use exceeded recharge by an estimated 2.5 times. Even today, amounts pumped still exceed recharge by more than twice. In 1972,

Nevada began to augment ground-water supplies by piping water from the Colorado River so that today ground-water pumping is the source for only 28 percent of Las Vegas's water use. Even with the addition of the Colorado River water, shortages are on the hori-

zon. The idea of a green lawn on each suburban home and a golf course down the street may soon be a thing of the past. However, it's important to note that nearly 90 percent of Nevada's water still goes to agriculture, and is used to irrigate hay for cattle. Considering that agriculture provides so few jobs, there undoubtedly will be a growing movement to divert this water towards urban use.

Recreation and Wilderness

Besides dropping quarters into the slots at casinos, Nevadans have almost unlimited opportunities for outdoor recreation. With everything from skiing the slopes to sailing on desert lakes to hiking in alpine wildernesses, Nevada has much to offer. And the best thing about these numerous mountains and deserts is that nearly all of the land is publicly owned, primarily by the federal government. In fact, 89.7 percent of Nevada is in federal ownership—a higher percentage than in any other state in the nation.

This public land endowment includes two national forests that take in the higher elevations of some of the state's most spectacular mountain ranges. The 3.7-million-acre Toiyabe (which includes some areas in California), the largest national forest outside of Alaska, covers portions of the Toiyabe Range,

Above: Highway 50, billed as the loneliest highway in America, traverses the central portion of Nevada, a land almost devoid of people. ***Top:*** *Irrigated alfalfa fields adjacent to the threatened Stillwater National Wildlife Refuge (see page 33).*

Monitor Range, Toquima Range, Carson Range by Reno, and the Spring Mountains near Las Vegas. The 2.5-million-acre Humboldt National Forest is spread over five units in northern and eastern Nevada and includes lands in the Snake Range, Schell Creek Range, Grant Range, Ruby Mountains, Quinn Canyon Range, Jarbidge and Santa Rosa Range, among others. A small sliver of the Inyo National Forest creeps into Nevada in the White Mountains.

Most of the national forests in Nevada were established to protect watershed quality and, other than fire wood, little timber is cut. The single greatest commercial use is domestic livestock grazing, which, ironically, has significantly affected watersheds throughout the forests. During the past five years, however, some individual ranger districts have made significant strides towards correcting or ending this abuse.

Most of the national forests in Nevada were established to protect watershed quality and, other than fire wood, little timber is cut.

In 1989 Congress expanded one wilderness area and designated 13 new ones. Together these areas cover fewer than 800,000 acres or approximately 1.03 percent of the state's 71 million acres of land. Wilderness areas are managed to retain their undeveloped characteristics. Recreation activities such as hunting, fishing, hiking, skiing and other non-motorized uses are permitted.

But the vast majority of public lands in Nevada is managed (or mismanaged as many critics might suggest) by the Bureau of Land Management, which has administrative jurisdiction over 47,956,000 acres or 68 percent of the Silver State. BLM lands include most valleys and many of the mountain ranges in Nevada. For the most part, BLM lands were parcels nobody else wanted after all the homesteading and mining claims, timber withdrawals, national forests and national parks were established. Today, you might call them the lands everyone wants. Many mining claims filed on public lands in Nevada are on BLM lands. In addition, nearly all the BLM lands in Nevada, some 45,256,419 acres,

are leased for livestock grazing. The BLM has recently inventoried and studied 111 roadless areas or WSA's (wilderness study areas) that total 5,125,418 acres. Not all of these, however, will be designated as protected wilderness.

Besides BLM and Forest Service lands, the National Park Service has several units in Nevada including a small portion of Death Valley National Monument, Great Basin National Park, and Lake Mead National Recreation Area.

Nevada also holds a number of national wildlife refuges managed by the U.S. Fish and Wildlife Service, including the 571,000-acre Sheldon National Wildlife Refuge in northeast Nevada, the 1.5-million-acre Desert Wildlife Refuge near Las Vegas, and a number of smaller refuges scattered around the state like the Stillwater, Ruby Lake, Ash Meadows, Anaho Island and Pahranagat.

Finally, the Department of Defense controls 4,145,039 acres or 5.9 percent of the total land area in Nevada. This includes Nellis Air Force Range, Tonopah Test Site and Hawthorne Ammunition Depot. These public lands are the foundation for Nevada's greatest asset—its space. The sense of freedom and quietude one feels looking out from a peak across range after range disappearing into the vast distance—that is Nevada's hidden mother lode. On a clear day, visibility may exceed 200 miles! Yet, time and time again while I was climbing some of Nevada's mountains, those distant views were obscured by smog coming from still more distant sources— mostly power plants in Utah and Arizona. While we have legislation to protect and preserve individual parcels of land as national parks or wilderness areas, it will be a shallow victory if, in the end, we can't preserve Nevada's sparkling air quality and its sense of space.

Above: Lake Mead by Boulder Beach, Lake Mead National Recreation Area. Lake Mead was created by damming the Colorado River.
Facing page: Nevada is dotted with ghost towns from its early mining years. Here, the yellow of rabbitbrush blooms amidst old mine buildings at Berlin in the Shoshone Range.

NEVADA GEOLOGY

Nevada is literally being pulled apart, and the mountains and valleys are fragments of the earth's crust that are sliding past each other.

Most of Nevada is considered to be part of the Basin and Range physiographic province. Basin and Range refers to repetition of fault-block mountains (horsts) bounded by valleys (grabens). The broad basins between the mountains are underlain by the same rock formations we see in the adjacent ranges, but are covered with debris and are not so readily visible. Although I shall focus on the Basin and Range province, two other physiographic regions lie on the state's fringes. North along the border of Idaho and Oregon lie the Owyhee Uplands, volcanic mesas and plateaus drained primarily by the Owyhee River and its tributaries. Along the very western edge of the state is the Sierra Nevada uplift, represented by the Carson Range.

The regular spacing of mountains and valleys typical of the Basin and Range is a consequence of the region's geological history, influenced by gigantic forces deep in the earth. Nevada is literally being pulled apart, and the mountains and valleys are fragments of the earth's crust that are sliding past each other. These crustal movements reveal a process known as plate tectonics.

Geological History

While we tend to believe that rocks are things that have substance and permanence, this is all a matter of perspective. In reality, rocks are continuously "dying" and being "reborn." The earth's surface is not really stable, but evolves and changes over time just as animal and plant species do. Entire ocean basins may become "extinct" and new ones form. Continents drift together and break apart. Plate tectonics theory tries to explain these changes. The theory suggests that the earth's crust is composed of no less than twenty plates—huge chunks of the earth's crust—that are drifting about, floating on the earth's mantle. The motion of these different plates relative to each other creates different geological formations and rock types.

The oldest rocks in the Great Basin lie near the border of Utah, Idaho and Nevada. Here, in the Grouse Creek Mountains, are schists that are 2.5 billion years old. Geologists theorize that about 2 billion years ago, the edge of an ancient North American plate was located here and an ocean once lapped at the edge of this land mass. Due to plate motion, about 1.75 billion years ago the ocean plate fronting on this edge of the North American continent began to subduct under the North American plate margin. As it dove deeper, the ocean plate melted, and molten rock shot upward through the overlying ocean basin crust to erupt as a series of volcanoes which formed an island arc something like the Aleutian Islands of today. But as the ocean plate continued to move under the North American plate, the island arc eventually was driven up against the continental mass and welded to the edge, thus extending the southern boundary of the continent southward into what is now the Great Basin and Nevada.

This process of adding new exotic continental crust (known as terranes) to existing plates is somewhat akin to taking a piece of clay and adding layer after layer of new clay of different colors, textures and chemical makeups. The various different origins of the terranes explains why rocks of radically different age, chemical makeup and geological origins can exist side by side. Most of the northwestern United States is made up of a series of such terranes.

About a billion years ago, another island arc of volcanoes was accreted onto the growing North American continental mass, extending its southern edge even farther south. In

Above: Volcanic boulders in the Goshute Mountains on Nevada's eastern border south of Wendover.

Left: Petrified sand dunes at Valley of Fire State Park in the Muddy Mountains of southern Nevada.

all, some 800 miles of new crust was added onto the continent as a result of these island arc collisions.

Sometime between 1.2 billion and 850 million years ago, part of the North American

Above: Cracked surface of a playa, or dried-up lake bed, Black Rock Desert near Gerlach. The white crust is made of salts left behind when the lake evaporated.

Top: Younger volcanic rock (dark rock in the background) covers older red sedimentary sandstone (exposed by erosion and seen in the foreground) in the Black Mountains, Lake Mead NRA.

continent ripped and separated right down the middle of what is now Nevada. An ocean basin developed in between the two continental fragments and today's central Nevada was once again ocean front property. This is one reason why the *sedimentary* limestones and other rocks in eastern and central Nevada differ dramatically from rocks found in western Nevada's granites, basalt or other *igneous*—or fire-caused—rocks.

At that time, the North American plate was much closer to the equator and a warm shallow sea developed between the two continental fragments. The eastern margin of the continent began to subside and a shallow ocean developed. Nearly 20,000 feet of carbonate sediments (which make limestone) were laid down in this ancient sea during this time. By this time, 570 million years ago, at the beginning of the Cambrian era, algae, trilobites (ancient shellfish) and other life was abundant in the seas. Their remains are preserved as fossils in the limestone rocks exposed today in central and eastern Nevada.

For millions of years, the sea continued to expand eastward, covering more and more of

what is now the Great Basin. Early forms of fish swam in these waters, and sediments from lands farther east flooded in. A huge area of tidal flats, reefs and beaches developed over much of the western United States.

Then, some geologists speculate, approximately 350 million years ago, about the time the first trees were developing on land, another offshore island arc complex began to move rapidly from the west toward the North American continental edge. It swallowed up the sea basin, and eventually collided with—and attached to—the western edge of the North American plate. The force of this movement buckled the sediments that had been on the sea floor and pushed them eastward, sometimes over older rock strata or between older layers. Deep-water rocks that had formed in ocean basins were thrust up and over younger shallow marine sediments. This thrust-faulting pushed rock layers more than 90 miles eastward. Known today as the Roberts Mountains Thrust Fault, it was named for the central Nevada mountains where the evidence for this great crustal movement is especially vivid. (See facing page.) But evidence for this thrust runs through central Nevada from the southwest to the northeast. Like rocks caught in a closing vise, many of the mountain ranges in central Nevada display severe compression, folding and deformity resulting from these intense pressures.

Some 235 million years ago, or well along the development of reptiles, the same general course of events repeated itself. Another island arc was rafted across the ocean basins to collide with the western edge of North America. Again, deep ocean sediments were thrust eastward 40 to 50 miles over younger, shallow-water deposits and sutured onto the North American plate. This large crustal movement, known as the Golconda Thrusts, is responsible for adding the exotic terrane that now makes up the northwestern third of Nevada.

Around the middle Jurassic, or approximately 160 million years ago, another microplate began to subduct under the western margin of North America. The compression and collision of the two plates pushed up a major mountain range along the continent's western edge. New exotic terranes accreted to North America enlarged it by 30 percent during this period. The collision also twisted the continent's western edge and thrust sediments of southern Nevada eastward. This is readily seen in Red Rock Canyon in the Spring Mountains near Las Vegas and in the Muddy Mountains at Lake Mead NRA. In both places, older limestone formations were thrust up and on top of younger layers of sandstone. Where the limestone cap has eroded away, sandstone now is exposed.

Beginning about 40 million years ago, a new ocean plate began to dive under the western edge of North America, creating a string of volcanoes that deposited great masses of volcanic material all over the northeastern portion of the Great Basin. Volcanic activity gradually spread southwest across Nevada. A huge volume of ash fused into tuff, or welded ash. Ash flows spread across the land, leveling valleys and basins into a huge featureless plain. Many of the mountains in the Great Basin are composed of ash and tuffs from this era of volcanic activity.

Then, about 17 million years ago, a great stretching of the earth's crust occurred between the Sierra Nevada in California and the Wasatch Range in Utah. In an area more than 1,000 miles long and as many as 600 miles wide, the earth's crust was cracked apart, creating north-south–trending faults where huge blocks of crust slid down relative to adjacent blocks' uplift. In many areas, the relief between the two crustal blocks was as much as 20,000 feet—three and a half miles. The Basin and Range had been created. Since that time, erosion has steadily removed much of the mountain surfaces, depositing them in the valleys. In some places, valley fill now is more than 10,000 feet in thickness.

What caused this crustal spreading and cracking is not known, although most geologists agree that some kind of heat source had risen beneath the Basin and Range region and caused an upward bowing of the earth's crust. The coincident timing of renewed volcanic activity across the region supports the theory of increased heat flow. Volcanic material poured out across the land in northern Nevada, eastern Oregon and southern Idaho, forming—among other things—the Snake River plain and the volcanic mesas and flows of northeast Nevada's highlands. Volcanic eruptions also produced calderas and volcanic cones in southern Nevada's Lincoln and Nye counties and within what is now Lake Mead NRA.

Glacial Landforms

The next touches put upon Nevada's mountains came about 2 million years ago at the start of the Pleistocene or Ice Age. Not only did the climate become cooler, but it was considerably wetter than at present. Treeline was lower, huge lakes flooded many of the valleys of the Great Basin, and small glaciers and ice caps crowned many of the higher mountain uplifts. Snow collected and, under pressure, turned to glacial ice. Once a glacier reaches 100 feet deep, the bottom becomes somewhat plastic and it begins to flow or ooze downhill—until melting at its terminus equals the input of fresh snow in the headwaters.

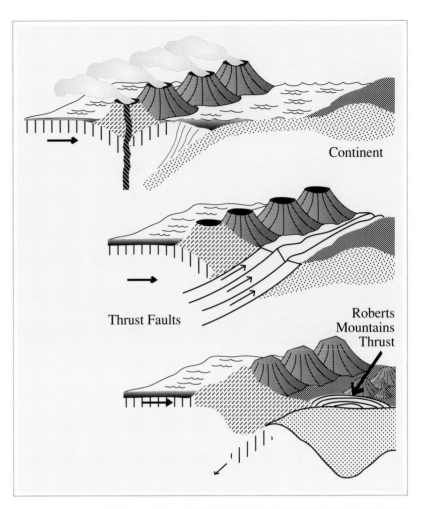

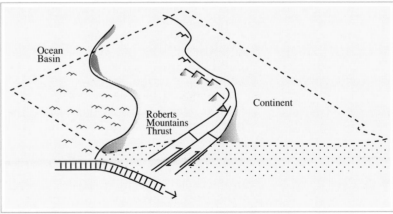

Top: *About 350 million years ago, some geologists speculate, a volcanic-island arc began to move eastward to attach to the North American continental plate.*

Bottom: *Like rocks caught in a closing vise, many of the mountain ranges in central Nevada display severe compression, folding and deformity resulting from those intense pressures. The Roberts Mountains Thrust Fault is named for the mountains where it is most evident.*

As a glacier grinds its way downslope, it scrapes the bottom and sides of valleys, steepens the angle of slopes and leaves behind U-shaped valley profiles. Lamoille Canyon in

the Ruby Mountains is a classic example of such a U-shaped glacial valley.

Small headwater sources for glaciers frequently carve bowl-shaped depressions known as cirques. The north side of Wheeler Peak in Great Basin National Park is a fine example of a glacial cirque. Lakes occupying such glacially carved basins are called cirque lakes. The Ruby Mountains and East Humboldt Mountains both have numerous examples of cirque lakes.

Constant abrasion from rubble and stones embedded in the bottom of the moving ice acts like sandpaper and smooths the rock surface, giving it a glacial polish.

Mountains that have been glaciated take on an angular, more rugged appearance. The Sierra on the western edge of the Great Basin in California has been heavily glaciated, as have the Ruby Mountains in Nevada. Other mountain areas with visible evidence of glaciation include the Spring Mountains near Las Vegas, the Toiyabe Range, East Humboldt Range, Carson Range, the Toquima Range, the Jarbidge Mountains, Santa Rosa Range, Independence Mountains, Schell Creek Range, and the Snake Range—location of Great Basin National Park. A cirque on Wheeler Peak's north face harbors the only remaining glacier in Nevada.

More obvious consequences of the Ice Age were the numerous large lakes that once flooded many of the Great Basin valleys. Two huge lakes occupied opposite sides of the region. Lake Bonneville covered most of northern Utah. Today, Great Salt Lake is a small remnant of it. Covering 45,000 square miles of northern and western Nevada was Lake Lahontan, of which Walker Lake and Pyramid Lake are relics. More than a hundred other smaller lakes also dotted the Great Basin. These lakes reached their peak about 12,000 years ago when Lake Lahontan had a maximum depth of 700 feet.

As the climate became more arid, many of these large lakes dried up and left behind huge, flat basins like Carson Sink, the Black Rock Desert and Smoke Creek Desert—all playas and relics of ancient Lake Lahontan. Other evidence for the ancient lakes includes old beach lines and dunes left after the water dried up.

Desert Landforms

Although we can't see it readily, Nevada's mountains still continue to change over time. Water is a major erosive factor, even in an arid climate like Nevada's. Many of the mountains have little vegetation to hold together the soil. When rain falls on these barren slopes, erosion is quite severe. Rushing water carries stone, silt and other debris down steep mountain canyons, dropping its load at the bottom. As sediments accumulate, the stream shifts back and forth across the outwash, forming a fan-shaped deposit known as an alluvial fan. When numerous alluvial fans are united, the more or less continuous apron that skirts the edge of the mountains is known as a bajada.

Another common feature of arid climates is differential erosion, especially of granite or quartzite rocks, into spherical shapes. Cracks or joints in the rock allow water to enter, then freeze-and-thaw cycles cause the rock to break apart. Over time, the result is a beach-ball–shaped rock formation.

Nevada's geological face is still changing as erosion tears down the mountains and the tectonic plates beneath our feet shift and move according to their internal clocks.

Above: Liberty Lake occupies a glacial cirque, or basin, carved by retreating glaciers that sculpted the Ruby Mountains near Elko. Ruby Mountains Wilderness, Humboldt National Forest.

Facing page: The horizontal layering of sedimentary formations is clearly seen in this eroded butte by Montana Agate Beach, Lake Mead National Recreational Area.

ASH MEADOWS
A LESSON IN ISLAND BIOGEOGRAPHY

Ash Meadows National Wildlife Refuge has the second greatest number of unique species of any site of its size in the country.

The 12,736-acre Ash Meadows National Wildlife Refuge was established in 1984 to protect one of the most biologically diverse sites in the United States. The refuge is 90 miles northeast of Las Vegas and just east of Death Valley on the California-Nevada border. It is an unassuming place; except for the presence of more than 30 warm water springs and numerous sloughs and seeps, it would not look appreciably different from the rest of the hundreds of thousands of square miles of desert surrounding it. But Ash Meadows has one of the highest levels of endemism (species that are unique to a particular area) in the entire continental United States and second highest of any known site of its size in North America.

This area holds a minimum of 26 species found nowhere else in the world. They include nine species of snails, six of plants, five fish species, two of insects and one mammal species. At least seven species of plant and four of fish, and several kinds of snails and insects are considered endangered under the Federal Endangered Species Act. One species, the Ash Meadows poolfish, already is extinct, victim of habitat modification that occurred only a decade or so ago.

The unusual number of unique species evolved over thousands of years. Approximately 12,000 years ago, the area around Ash Meadows was much lusher and a large lake filled the Amargosa Valley. As the climate dried, species like the endemic fish found at Ash Meadows became isolated in individual springs. Over time, they evolved into unique species. For example, three fish species—the Devils Hole pupfish, Warm Springs pupfish and Ash Meadows Amargosa pupfish—are probably all descendents of one ancestor. But as water levels dropped and the pluvial lake dried up, the original ancestors of each of these kinds of fish became isolated in a different spring, with no opportunities to interbreed. Effectively, these were aquatic islands set amidst a sea of desert. Segregated, each population of pupfish evolved in isolation, rapidly evolving into a new and different species.

Ash Meadows was first given special status in 1952 when a 40-acre tract surrounding the site of Devils Hole, a pool no more than 55 by 10 feet, was added to Death Valley National Monument. Here lives the entire world's population of the Devils Hole pupfish—its population fluctuating between 150 and 700 individuals.

The rest of the area, however, lacked any kind of protection. In the 1960s, peat was mined in Carson Slough, destroying 2,000 acres of prime wetland habitat. Then in the 1970s an elaborate cattle ranching venture supplied by irrigated hay fields was begun. Dams and irrigation canals were built and ground water pumping (mining) began to lower the area's springs. The water flowing from Ash Meadow springs is considered "fossil water" which was deposited in the aquifer some 12,000 years ago.

As the water table dropped, the National Park Service stepped in to protect the Devils Hole pupfish. The first negotiations tried to arrange some minimum water level. Unsuccessful at this first attempt, the Park Service eventually went to court and won a minimum water standard. The ranching operation was put up for sale and bought by a Las Vegas development company that planned to build a resort and subdivision with 20,000 homes in the meadows. As roads began to riddle the meadows, and springs were altered to divert flows, the Nature Conservancy stepped in to seek a land trade or conservation easements. None of these efforts were successful. Finally, an emergency appropriation by Congress permitted the purchase of these biologically critical lands; The Nature Conservancy acted as intermediary, arranging a sale to the U.S. Fish and Wildlife Service.

NEVADA'S 26 HIGHEST MOUNTAIN RANGES WITH PEAKS OVER 10,000 FEET

Range	Highest Peak in Range	Elev. Feet
Antelope Range	Ninemile Peak	10,104
Carson Range	Mt. Rose	10,776
Cherry Creek Range	Head of Goshute Canyon	10,458
Diamond Mountains	Diamond Peak	10,614
East Humboldt Range	Hole-in-the-Mountain Peak	11,306
Egan Range	South Ward Mountain	10,936
Grant Range	Troy Peak	11,298
Hot Creek Range	Morey Peak	10,246
Independence Mtns.	McAffee Peak	10,439
Jarbidge Mtns.	Matterhorn	10,839
Monitor Range	Monitor Mountain	10,888
Pequop Mountains	Spruce Mountain	10,262
Pilot Range	Pilot Peak	10,716
Quinn Canyon Range	Ridge west of Pine Creek	10,229
Roberts Mountains	Roberts Creek Mountain	10,133
Ruby Mountains	Ruby Dome	11,387
Schell Creek Range	North Schell Peak	11,883
Shoshone Range	North Shoshone Peak	10,313
Snake Range	Wheeler Peak	13,063
Spring Mountains	Charleston Peak	11,912
Sweetwater Mtns.	Middle Sister*	10,600
Toiyabe Range	Arc Dome	11,788
Toquima Range	Mt. Jefferson	11,941
Wassuk Range	Mt. Grant	11,239
White Mountains	Boundary Peak*	13,140
White Pine Range	Currant Mountain	11,512

*Highest in the Nevada portion of these ranges. In California, Mt. Patterson (11,673 feet) is the highest peak in the Sweetwater Range, and White Mountain Peak (14,246 feet) highest of the White Mountains.

Information compiled from U.S. Geological Survey topographic maps and Alvin McLane's Silent Cordilleras.

Moonrise over Spruce Mountain, north of Currie.

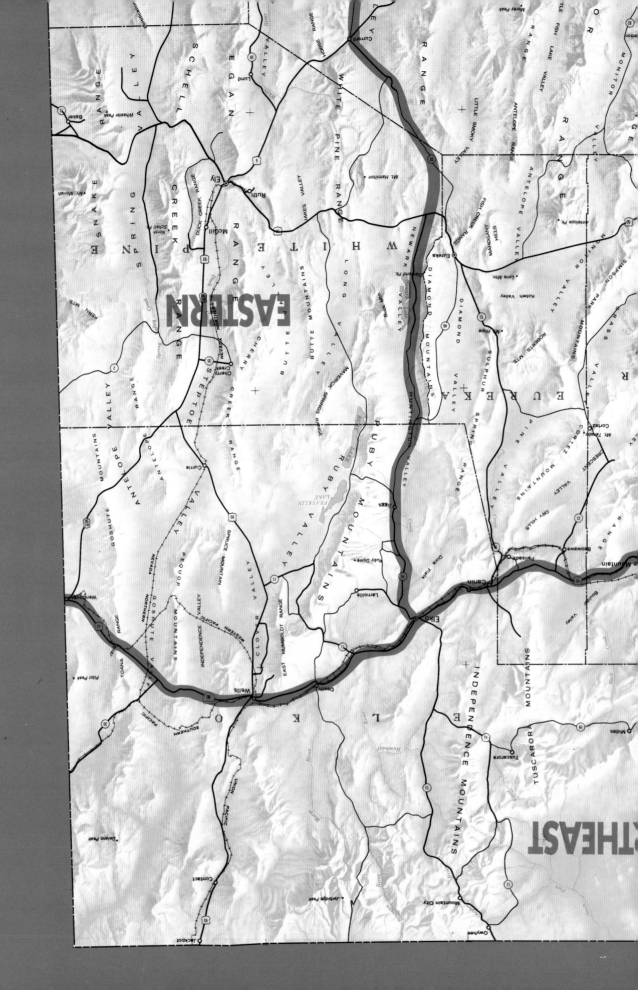

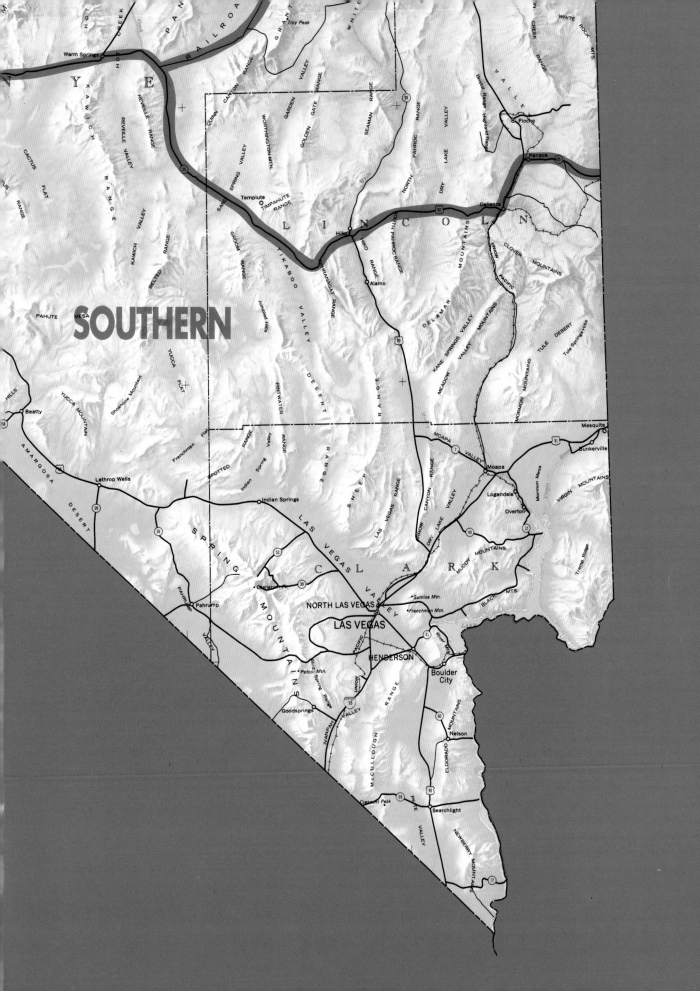

SOUTHERN

Bunker Hill in the Toiyabe Range is Nevada's 18th-highest named peak at 11,464 feet.

NEVADA'S 31 HIGHEST NAMED PEAKS

All above 11,000 feet in Elevation

Name	Elevation	Range
Boundary Peak	13,140	White Mountains
Wheeler Peak	13,063	Snake Range
Jeff Davis Peak	12,771	Snake Range
Mt. Baker	12,298	Snake Range
Mt. Moriah	12,067	Snake Range
Mt. Jefferson	11,941	Toquima Range
Pyramid Peak	11,926	Snake Range
Charleston Peak	11,918	Spring Mountains
North Schell Peak	11,883	Schell Creek Range
Arc Dome	11,788	Toiyabe Range
South Schell Peak	11,735	Schell Creek Range
Taft Mountain	11,705	Schell Creek Range
Mt. Washington	11,676	Snake Range
Lincoln Peak	11,597	Snake Range
Bald Mountain	11,562	Snake Range
Mummy Mountain	11,530	Spring Mountains
Currant Mountain	11,513	White Pine Range
Bunker Hill	11,464	Toiyabe Range
Ruby Dome	11,387	Ruby Mountains
Toiyabe Dome	11,361	Toiyabe Range
Thomas Peak	11,316	Ruby Mountains
Hole-in-the-Mtn. Peak	11,306	East Humboldt Range
Troy Peak	11,298	Grant Range
Mt. Grant	11,239	Wassuk Range
Granite Peak	11,213	Snake Range
Duckwater Peak	11,188	White Pine Range
Verdi Peak	11,074	Ruby Mountains
Griffith Peak	11,072	Spring Mountains
King Peak	11,031	Ruby Mountains
Lee Peak	11,025	Ruby Mountains
Humboldt Peak	11,020	East Humboldt Range

Limber pine below Chimney Rock in East Humboldt Range. East Humboldt Wilderness in Humboldt National Forest near Wells.

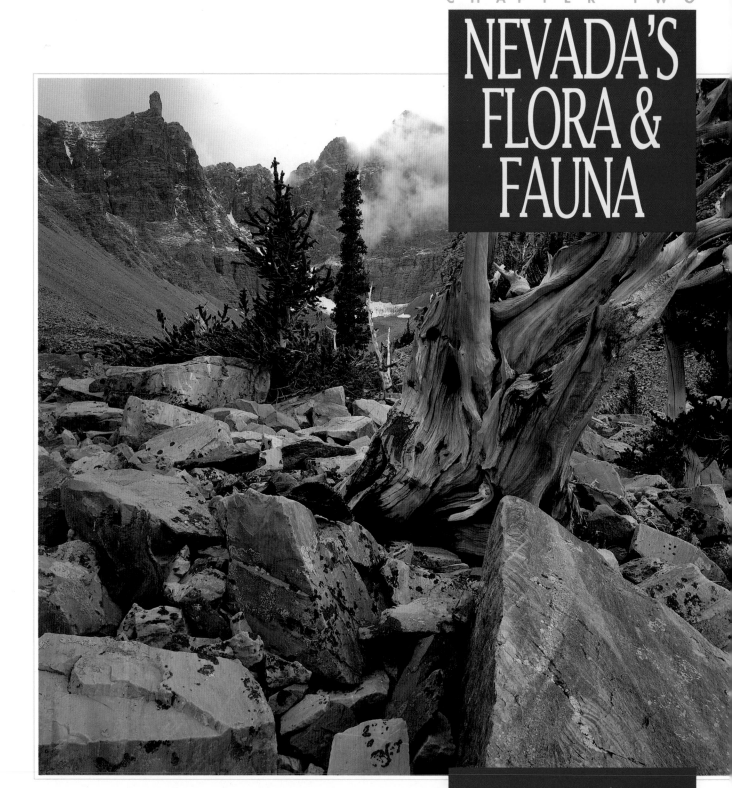

CHAPTER TWO

NEVADA'S FLORA & FAUNA

Nevada has one of the most
diverse flora and fauna
assemblages in
the United States.

I t may come as a surprise to some who view Nevada as nothing but a gray veneer of sagebrush, but the state has one of the most diverse flora and fauna assemblages in the United States, with a high degree of endemic, or exclusively native, plants. Only California, Texas, Hawaii and Florida have greater biodiversity. The reason for such diversity is easy to understand if you consider that many of the mountain ranges are like islands surrounded by a sea of desert. Each island permits the evolution of genetically isolated species, which over time evolve into unique and new animals or plants. Island biogeography is the name given such diversification by isolation. Small land masses—like islands in the sea—cannot support as large and diverse populations as larger land masses. Smaller populations result in reduced competition, and chance fluctuations or mutations in the genetic code spread quickly throughout the population. The Galapagos, Hawaiian Islands and other oceanic islands are famous for their unusual and even unique wildlife and plant species—a consequence of their "islandness."

In a similar manner, the mountains, basins and waterways of the Great Basin are essentially islands, each with unique combinations of plants and animals that chanced to colonize and survive there. For instance, the Jarbidge Mountains have subalpine fir forests—but no Douglas fir, which is common in mountain ranges farther east in Utah. West of

the Jarbidge lies the Pine Forest Range and the only conifer found there is whitebark pine, typically a subalpine species common in the northern Rockies and the Sierra. The Santa Rosa Range, which lies between the Jarbidge Mountains and Pine Forest Range, has no subalpine fir nor whitebark pine, but has scattered stands of limber pine. Each is an example of an "island" amid a sea of desert with a depauperate tree species diversity.

Another general principle of island biogeography is that islands closer to the mainland have more species than islands farther out to sea. For Nevada, consider the mainland "continental" mass to be the Sierra and the Rockies. The Carson Range, then, with no real barriers separating its forests from those of the main crest of the Sierra, has a forest assemblage nearly as rich. Tree species found in the Carson Range include Utah juniper, singleleaf pinyon pine, curlleaf mountain mahogany, ponderosa pine, Jeffrey pine, Washoe pine, white and red fir, western juniper, mountain hemlock, western white pine, lodgepole pine and whitebark pine.

Farther from the Sierra "mainland" is the Virginia Range. It has western white pine, white fir, lodgepole pine, whitebark pine, along with ponderosa pine, Jeffrey pine, Utah juniper, pinyon, and mahogany. Beyond the Lahontan trough lying east of the Virginia Range, no exclusively Sierran conifers occur.

Isolated central Nevada ranges like the Toiyabe and Monitor ranges typically have two to three tree species associated with them—usually aspen, limber pine and bristlecone pine.

No pinyon pine grows north of the Humboldt River, and even juniper is scarce. Why? Perhaps these species simply haven't had enough time to colonize these areas since the close of the last Ice Age, or changing climatic conditions so reduced existing populations that they were locally extirpated.

On the eastern side of Nevada we see a trend similar to that of the west's Sierran forests. The farther west one gets from the Wasatch Front, which is the last outlier of the Rocky Mountain "continental" mass, the few-

Above: The golden eagle, Nevada's largest raptor, is found throughout the state, but its greatest densities occur in the state's northern third. Biologists estimate that Nevada may support as many as 1,200 nesting pairs.

Left: Bristlecone pine below Wheeler Peak, Great Basin National Park. Bristlecone pine are among the oldest living trees in the world. Associated with timberline locations on the higher mountain ranges of eastern and southern Nevada, they may live for as long as 5,000 years.

Above: Clark's nut-crackers extract pine nuts and cache the seeds for future use, both ensuring the bird's survival when food is scarce and helping to distribute the heavy seeds of pine trees.

Top right: Bighorn sheep are distributed throughout the state's mountain areas, with three varieties known in Nevada—desert, California, and Rocky Mountain bighorn. The desert variety is the most numerous.

Right: Elk were native to the eastern portion of the state, but were extirpated by overhunting. They have been reintroduced into a number of mountain ranges within their former range, as well as in new areas such as the Monitor Range and Spring Mountains.

er tree species one encounters. The Snake Range, for example, harbors 11 tree species: Utah juniper, pinyon pine, ponderosa pine, Douglas fir, mountain mahogany, white fir, Engelmann spruce, aspen, limber pine, lodgepole pine, and bristlecone pine. But just a little farther west, Rocky Mountain species such as Engelmann spruce, Douglas fir and ponderosa pine disappear.

The more isolated mountain ranges in Nevada tend to have fewer plant species, but they have fewer bird species as well. Since birds can fly, this may seem puzzling at first; birds, however, need habitat diversity to provide for all their needs. If there are fewer plant species, the lower habitat diversity supports fewer birds.

This principle is also evident in mammal distributions. Ten typically Sierran mammals found in the Carson Range are absent from the Virginia Range, just one mountain range to the east. These include black bear, snowshoe hare, northern flying squirrel, mountain pocket gopher, Townsend's chipmunk, mountain beaver, marten, lodgepole chipmunk, and long-eared chipmunk. The same depauperate, or less than is possible, mammal distribution is seen on the eastern edge of Nevada as well. Mammals typical of dense forest—like snowshoe hare, marten, northern flying squirrel and black bear—are missing.

So what happened to all these species? Why no black bear, pine marten, red squirrel or snowshoe hare in the Pine Nut Range or Rubies? One possibility is that these species never came to these areas. But perhaps the answer lies in another principle of island biogeography: small populations are much more likely to go extinct than larger ones, due to random extinctions. Since small islands hold fewer individuals than large ones, they often have fewer than the minimum number of individuals for a viable population. Once a population goes below this number, the chances are reduced that it will be able to produce enough young to replace those dead from disease, starvation, predation or random population fluctuations.

This principle was recently documented by Dr. Joel Berger, a professor at the University of Nevada, Reno. Berger compiled a list of all bighorn sheep populations in the state and found that herds with fewer than 50 individuals went extinct within 50 years. Thus, it would seem that 50 sheep is the very minimum for a viable population.

Perhaps the most interesting example of isolation and speciation (development into new species), as well as extinction, is seen in Nevada's population of fishes. With the exception of the Colorado River along the state's southern border, and a few tributaries of the

Snake in the northern part of the state, all of Nevada's watersheds are isolated systems. They flow into desert sinks and disappear. As a consequence, this desert state has 67 endemic species of fishes—kinds found nowhere else in the world. And since nearly all rivers, springs and aquifers are tapped and dewatered (primarily for agricultural production) Nevada also holds the dubious distinction of having more endangered fish species than any other state in the nation! At least seven species of fishes are extinct throughout their range, and another four are no longer found in Nevada although they still occur outside of the state.

Exacerbating the problem is the introduction of exotic fishes, usually sport species. So many non-native types of fishes (63 species) have been introduced into Nevada state waters that only 58 percent of the fish species and subspecies found in the state are natives.

A Desert State

Nevada is the most desert-like of all the states. Nearly all of its lower elevations are considered deserts. This means they receive little annual precipitation, and that the amount of percipitation is more erratic than in non-desert areas. For instance, recent research in eastern Oregon, just north of the Nevada border found that annual precipitation was, on the average, below normal one in five years. Plants and animals living here need to be able to adjust to periodic and frequent years of below-normal moisture. However, our perception of what is "normal" may need revision. As one ecologist noted, the arid West does not experience drought, but more precisely, it has occasional periods of excess moisture.

More importantly for living things, evaporation rates range between 45 and 90 inches a year. What this means is the air could absorb 90 inches of water annually—if it were there to absorb. Approximately 600,000 acre-feet of water is evaporated annually from Lake Mead alone. This is more water than most reservoirs hold.

Surviving under such circumstances means

Cactus wren constructing its nest in a cholla cactus. Cactus wrens are found in southern Nevada's Mojave desert.

plants and animals must adopt survival strategies that reduce water loss. Some, such as the kangaroo rat and many other rodents, spend their days inside burrows where average humidity is much higher than outside, ven-

Above: Wildflowers in Lamoille Canyon, the Ruby Mountains.

turing forth only at night when evaporation rates are lower. Many plants have adopted a strategy of small leaves, reducing evaporation losses and decreasing the surface area that can be heated to excessive temperatures. Some plants, such as sagebrush, even develop several sets of leaves. Larger leaves grow during the spring when soil moisture is higher, but are dropped and replaced by smaller ones that stay through the drought of summer.

The cacti have taken this a step further and have no leaves at all! Instead, their stems and pads hold chlorophyll to photosynthesize food.

A Tale of Two Deserts

Nevada has two major desert biomes—Great Basin and Mojave Desert. The Mojave Desert lies in the southern part of the state surrounding Las Vegas. Biologically, it is an exceedingly rich area compared to regions farther north. Although comprising only one sixth of the state's area, it is home to 43 percent of all species recorded in the state.

The Mojave, most of which is in California, is the smallest of the four major desert types found in North America. Generally lower in elevation, it is warmer than the central and northern parts of the state. Precipitation is highest in the western part of the Mo-

jave and gradually diminishes to the east, with much of southern Nevada getting fewer than three inches of precipitation annually—mostly in the winter months. Although snow occasionally falls, it never lasts more than a day or two. The Amargosa "River" is the only waterway in this region (excluding the Colorado, which does not originate here) and it empties into Death Valley and disappears.

Characteristic plants include creosote bush at lower elevations with Joshua tree and other yuccas dominating higher elevations. Cacti occur here but are less abundant than in the Sonoran Desert of Arizona.

The rest of Nevada is part of the Great Basin Desert. The Great Basin is the largest and coldest of the North America deserts. Snow is frequent, as are freezing temperatures. Most precipitation comes in late winter and spring months, while summers are hot and dry.

The most characteristic plant species is sagebrush, which occupies at least 45 percent of the Great Basin. In some places, like the Santa Rosa Range, sagebrush may cover mountains all the way up to the 10,000-foot level. If you're rolling across Nevada through a dun-colored landscape, you're probably in the Great Basin. But, although they may all look the same, there are actually 12 species of sagebrush in the West—more, if you consider subspecies.

Major Plant Communities

Let's traverse the major plant communities one will likely encounter in Nevada, beginning at the lowest elevations and working up to the tops of the highest peaks.

Riparian Zones. Because most of Nevada is classified as desert, the riparian zones are biologically the most important habitat here, supporting 70 to 80 percent of animal species on only one percent of the land. Riparian areas are the thin green corridors adjacent to streams or waterways, where

Above: Moonrise over rabbitbrush and sagebrush, typical plants of the Great Basin, seen here near Currie.

water is abundant and lush vegetation dominates. Where they occur, the largest deciduous tree is usually one of three species of cottonwood. Frémont cottonwood is the most common species, but black cottonwood is found

Paintbrush growing in limestone of the Snake Creek Canyon.
JEFF GNASS PHOTO

in the western ranges and in a few northern ranges like the Jarbidge Mountains and Santa Rosa Range. Narrowleaf cottonwood grows at higher elevations in the Schell Creek and Monitor ranges, and the Spring, Jarbidge and Ruby mountains. In the understory of cottonwood, one finds a host of small trees and shrubs, including Wood's rose, alder, water birch, red osier dogwood, willows, chokecherry, elderberry, serviceberry and a host of smaller shrubs and grasses.

Riparian areas occupy only about 1 percent of Nevada, but this limited extent belies their biological importance. One study in eastern Oregon documented that 80 percent of the 363 terrestrial vertebrate species relied upon the riparian community for survival, or preferred it more than any other habitat.

Birds typically associated with these zones include western kingbirds, yellow warblers, song sparrows and yellow-breasted chats populating stream-side thickets, marsh wrens living in cattail marshes, and northern harriers skimming wet meadows in search of prey.

Despite their biological importance, riparian zones have faired poorly. Dams, water diversions, and livestock grazing have all taken their toll and have caused a tremendous lessening in Nevada's biological diversity. For instance, in 1868, U.S. Geological Survey crew member Robert Ridgeway did an inventory of birds along the Truckee River. He described the river as supporting exceedingly dense willows, with many side sloughs filled with rushes. Cottonwood groves lined the river, with beautiful meadowlands along the banks and extending across the valley. A hundred years later, much had changed. The sloughs were channelized, the stream sides and meadows destroyed by overgrazing and development. When resurveyed between 1972 and 1981 by University of Nevada biologists, they found only 49 of the 91 breeding bird species Ridgeway had reported. Furthermore, the populations of 26 of those 49 that remained had declined significantly.

Creosote Bush Zone. One of the identifying plants of the Mojave Desert portion of Nevada is creosote bush. These large evergreen shrubs form almost continuous, widely-spaced stands. Mixed with this shrub are bursage, brittlebush, spiny hopsage and skeleton weed. At higher elevations, one finds blackbrush and Joshua tree. Cacti such as beavertail, prickly pear, barrel and cholla are also common in some locations. Grasses include Indian ricegrass, squirreltail, desert muhly, dropseed, and galleta grass. One of the interesting distributional oddities is the occurrence of Joshua tree in the Delamar Mountains, where it grows amidst sagebrush almost into the juniper woodlands.

Wildlife residents of the creosote bush zone include the roadrunner, desert tortoise, desert bighorn sheep, gray fox, Merriman kangaroo rat, Gambel quail, black-throated sparrow, verdin, Le Conte thrasher, poor will, cactus wren, ringtail cat, antelope ground squirrel and bobcat.

Of the larger mammals, bighorn sheep are perhaps most prized to see, since they are relatively rare. Typically they are found associated with steep, rugged terrain, although not necessarily confined to the creosote bush zone. In fact, they can be found associated with nearly every major plant community in Nevada, all the way up to timberline. They eat both grass and shrubs.

Bighorn sheep were probably the most widely *distributed* larger mammal when Europeans first explored the area, but even then were not numerous. Nevertheless, it is thought that their numbers were much greater then than today. Unregulated hunting by settlers, forage competition and disease from domestic livestock nearly wiped out this animal over much of its historic range.

Studies by the Nevada Department of Wildlife document that sheep populations are considerably lower where cattle grazing is permitted, averaging only 0.88 sheep per square mile, whereas ungrazed areas have more than 2.54 sheep per square mile. There are no bighorn populations wherever domestic sheep graze. This is one reason why southern Nevada, with its limited domestic livestock grazing, is home to 95 percent of the state's bighorn sheep.

Based on horn characteristics, body size, coat color and other features, some biologists divide Nevada's wild sheep into three varieties: desert bighorn, found in central and southern Nevada desert ranges; California bighorn, native to western and northwest Nevada along the California border; and Rocky Mountain bighorn in the eastern part of the state.

Since 1968, when Nevada began a bighorn reintroduction program, more than 1,219 sheep have been transplanted to 42 different sites in the state. Today an estimated 5,200 desert bighorns occupy 37 ranges in southern Nevada, while California bighorn and Rocky Mountain bighorn number fewer than 500.

Shadscale Zone. Within the Great Basin portion of the state three major plant communities—shadscale, sagebrush, and pinyon-juniper—blanket the valleys and lower slopes of the mountains. Collectively, they cover about 75 percent of the region.

At the lowest, hottest elevation, where soils tend to be salty and precipitation is less than 7 inches annually, lies the shadscale zone. It dominates two broad areas below 4,500 feet in Nevada. Near Tonopah, it forms an intermediate zone between the creosote deserts to the south and sagebrush of the north. Farther north, it is particularly noticeable in the Lahontan Basin, which includes the old lake bed of glacial Lake Lahontan in northwest Nevada.

Although shadscale will sometimes form pure stands, in most cases it grows alongside several other species including greasewood, winterfat, bud sage, four-winged saltbush, broom snakeweed, Nuttall's saltbush and sticky rabbitbrush.

Small rodents are fairly common in this zone and include the chisel-toothed kangaroo rat, which feeds almost exclusively on shadscale. Other kangaroo rats include the desert kangaroo rat and Ord's kangaroo rat. Also found in this zone are badger, kit fox, coyote,

Botta's pocket gopher, montane vole, long-tailed pocket mouse, antelope ground squirrels, blacktailed jackrabbit and least chipmunks.

Sagebrush Zone. At slightly higher elevations, usually above 5,000 feet, where precipitation is greater than 7 inches, lies the sagebrush zone dominated by *Artemisia tridentata* or big sagebrush. Associated with big sagebrush are other sagebrush species such as low sagebrush in the north, and black sagebrush to the east and south, as well as antelope bitterbrush, hopsage and rabbitbrush.

Prior to the introduction of livestock and widespread adoption of fire suppression, this zone was co-dominated by grasses such as bluebunch wheatgrass, Idaho fescue, Great Basin wild rye, and needle and thread grass. Measurements of protected areas show that a typical sagebrush stand is 73 percent grasses, and sagebrush usually makes up only about 15 percent of the ground cover. In some areas, elimination of livestock grazing coupled with prescribed burns has resulted in a luxurious recreation of these former grassland-shrub mixtures.

Associated with the sagebrush zone are sage grouse, sage sparrow, sage thrasher, Brewer's sparrow, mourning dove, least chipmunk, sage vole, kit fox, coyote, badger, bobcat, northern grasshopper mouse and pygmy cottontail. But by far the most abundant species

Above: Blacktail jackrabbit.

Top: The kit fox is a seldom seen, nocturnal desert dweller found in valleys in the southern deserts and the low valleys associated with the Lahontan trough area of western Nevada.

is the black-tailed jackrabbit, whose biomass, or volume of living creatures, in some areas surpasses that of all rodents combined. Birds of prey that seek out jackrabbits include golden eagles and red-tailed hawks.

Among larger mammals, only mule deer and antelope are commonly associated with this zone. Antelope are perhaps unique in that they feed on sagebrush nearly year-round, although non-grass herbs are important to them in summer months.

In North America as a whole, antelope once numbered in the millions, rivaling the bison for sheer numbers. As a consequence of both overhunting and competition from domestic livestock, however, this species declined to a record low of 10,000 over its entire North American range by 1918. Since then, its numbers have increased, but populations are still less than one one-hundredth of their former numbers.

Although present in Nevada, antelope never were abundant. In 1990, Nevada had an estimated 18,500 antelope, most concentrated in the northern plateau region, including the Sheldon National Wildlife Refuge that was specifically set aside to protect antelope and their habitat.

In North America as a whole, antelope once numbered in the millions, rivaling the bison for sheer numbers.

Pinyon-Juniper Zone. Scattered along the base of many Nevada mountain ranges—usually between 6,000 and 9,000 feet—is a zone of short, squat trees, rarely taller than 20 feet in height, forming an open woodland: the pinyon-juniper zone. This woodland type occupies more of Nevada's mountains than any other, and is typically associated with areas where annual precipitation exceeds 12 inches.

Singleleaf pinyon pine and Utah juniper are the dominant species with juniper usually occupying the lower elevations and pinyon pine occupying slightly higher areas. For some reason, parts of northern Nevada, including the Santa Rosa, Black Rock and Pine Forest ranges, have neither juniper nor pinyon pine. An unusual ecotype of juniper called "swamp cedar" occupies the lowest portions of Spring Valley between the Snake Range and Schell Creek Range in eastern Nevada.

Prior to the advent of livestock, pinyon-juniper woodlands were mostly confined to rocky areas where lack of fuel gave trees some protection from relatively frequent wildfires. Overgrazing by domestic livestock eliminated many of the fine fuels associated with grasses and led to a reduction in fire frequency throughout the Great Basin. As a consequence, the pinyon-juniper zone has expanded its range in many areas. For example, recent research in Great Basin National Park has shown the average age for mature trees on a rocky slope was 400 to 470 years. On less rocky sites, nearly all trees were found to be less than 100 years in age, corresponding roughly to the time when heavy livestock grazing was introduced in this area, and the high tide of timbering for the first mining boom.

In addition, these woodland expansions (called "invasions" by livestock advocates) may be responding to changing global climatic conditions. since the end of the Little Ice Age in 1850, temperatures in the West have warmed, perhaps allowing greater expansion of the pinyon and juniper woodlands in the region.

Whatever the cause for woodland increase, ranchers don't like pinyon-juniper forests because they offer less livestock forage. Since almost all ranchers believe the only reason public land exists is to feed their cows, a rangeland with expanding woodlands is seen as a threat. Using their considerable political clout to get the government to do something about the "invasion" (they would never pay for anything like this themselves), the managing agencies responded by implementing a plant community conversion. How? Get two bulldozers, tie an anchor chain between them and violently rip out the trees.

Between 1960 and 1972, more than a third of a million acres of pinyon-juniper forest in Utah and Nevada was destroyed by this method. What impacts this had on woodland ecosystems no one knows. One thing is certain: in most cases, this method provided no long-term solution, since the same major factors that led to the "invasion"—namely overgrazed rangelands and fire suppression—still exist.

Certainly the wildlife that depends upon these species do not see this woodland expansion as an "invasion." Pinyon pines have large nuts that are both tasty and nutritious. Nevada Indian tribes depended on the nuts for winter survival, as did many smaller mammals and birds, including the ubiquitous pinyon jay. The pinyon jay extracts pine nuts from the cone and then caches them in the

Above: Tall ponderosa pine stands high above the shorter and stouter pinyon pine along Lehman Creek in Great Basin National Park. Ponderosas are found in scattered locations among the mountains of southern, eastern and western Nevada, but not in the central and north-western mountains.

Facing page: An estimated 18,500 antelope are thought to inhabit Nevada, primarily in the northern portion of the state.

ground, ensuring itself a winter-spring food supply, and at the same time helping to distribute the pinyon seed.

Other animals one encounters in pinyon-juniper woodlands include bushtit, plain tit-

Wheeler Peak Bristlecone Pine Grove, Great Basin National Park. JEFF GNASS PHOTO

mouse, robin, Townsend's solitaire, cliff chipmunk, porcupine, bobcat, mule deer, bighorn sheep, mountain lion, coyote and pinyon mouse.

Many Nevada mountain ranges have stands of another shrubby tree that lies even higher than the pinyon-juniper belt—mountain mahogany. Woodlands of these trees, with their wide-spreading crowns, look something like acadia tree savannas in Africa. Mahogany is an important winter food for mule deer.

Mid-Elevation Forests. Generalizations about forests in the Great Basin are difficult because tree distribution is spotty at best. As mentioned previously, the closer you get to either the Sierra or the Rockies, the more tree species occur.

Perhaps the most widespread species in Nevada's mountains is aspen. Deciduous trees with beautiful, smooth, white bark, groves of aspen form brilliant patches of gold in autumn. The species is fairly abundant in most of the higher mountain ranges of Nevada.

Aspens rarely reproduce from seed. Instead, their roots send up thousands of suckers, each of which may become a "new" tree. But since neighboring suckers are all joined by the same root system, many aspen groves are genetically related—all members of the same clone. They leaf out in the spring at the same time,

turn color in the fall simultaneously, and drop their leaves all at once. If you see a hillside of aspen in the fall, the different clones are often easy to pick out, with one group still green while another, adjacent clone may be golden.

Aspens depend upon disturbance for survival. Typically, a fire burns through a grove, eliminating the above-ground stems. This triggers the production of new suckers and rejuvenation of the grove. Since this has been repeated over and over for thousands of years, some aspen clones may date back to the last Ice Age.

Although aspen is relatively widespread, most conifers have a more restricted distribution. Ponderosa pine is known from a few ranges like the Carson, Virginia and Pah Rah in the west and from the Snake, Wilson Creek and Quinn Canyon Ranges in the east. It also grows in southern Nevada ranges like the Mormon, Clover, and Spring mountains near Las Vegas. Subalpine fir is known only from the Jarbidge, Independence and Bull Run Mountains in northeastern Nevada. Engelmann spruce, a Rocky Mountain species, is abundant in the Pilot, Schell Creek and Snake ranges, although one small stand is also reported for the Ruby Mountains near Elko. And Douglas fir, another Rocky Mountain colonizer, occurs only in the Snake, Schell Creek, Wilson Creek and White Pine ranges of eastern Nevada.

White fir has two varieties. One has been a major component of the Tahoe Basin forest, although it is dying as a consequence of drought and disease, exacerbated by fire suppression. The other grows in the Sierra, where it is found in the Carson Range. It extends only into eastern Nevada and grows in the Grant, Snake, Schell Creek, Pilot, Pequop and Toana ranges. The Spring Mountains near Las Vegas also have extensive stands of white fir.

Wildlife associated with the mid-elevation forest zone vary with the tree species of each range, as well as with the species' colonization and extinction rates, but some generalization can still be made. In some of the eastern Nevada ranges like the Schell Creek and Egan ranges, elk are fairly common, with small numbers also found in the Jarbidge Mountains, Pilot Range, Monitor Range, and Spring Mountains. Mule deer are widely distributed. Along aspen-lined creeks, beavers are common, and one will find goshawks nesting in the trees . Other birds of this zone include mountain bluebird, sharp-shinned hawk, Cooper's hawk, northern flicker, black-billed magpie, and mountain chickadee.

Timberline Forests. At the highest elevations on many Nevada mountains one will find scattered forests of three pine species—

limber, whitebark and bristlecone. However, in most instances, only one or at most two of these three species will be encountered in any particular range, although in Thomas Canyon in the Ruby Mountains, all three species are known to occur.

As a rule, bristlecone pine dominates on mountains in southern Nevada, while limber pine is more common in northern Nevada. Whitebark pine is known only in a few mountain areas of Nevada—the Ruby Mountains, Independence Mountains, and East Humboldt and Pine Forest ranges. Where the two grow together, whitebark typically grows in the higher and wetter areas.

Both limber and whitebark pine are dependent upon Clark's nutcracker for their continued existence. Both pines have large, nutritious seeds that are an attractive food source to the nutcracker. Gathering seeds while the cones are still green, the birds cache them here and there for future use, thus ensuring a food supply in winter and spring, when seeds are unavailable. But the bird seldom recovers all its cached seeds, and the "left-over" seeds sprout to make new trees. Thus both bird and tree benefit from the relationship.

While limber pine and whitebark pine will often take on the gnarled and twisted demeanors of seemingly ancient age, they seldom live more than 400 to 500 years. The title for longevity easily goes to the bristlecone pine, which is known to live almost 5,000 years. No one knows why they live so long—or, as one person suggested, just take so long to die—but the oldest trees grow on the least productive sites.

One adaptation for long life is the bristlecone's ability to retain needles for as many as forty years. This means they expend less energy producing new needles every few years (unlike most conifers). Another factor in their long life may be related to climatic conditions. The dry air and cool temperatures near timberline slow decomposition. Furthermore, bristlecone pine is full of resins that help preserve its wood. This means the tree will remain standing for centuries even after most of it has died. Often all that remains alive is a tiny strip of bark connecting a few branches with a few needles to the root system.

Bristlecone pine is abundant in eastern Nevada's calcareous mountains like Spruce Mountain, and the Schell Creek, Snake, Egan, Quinn Canyon, and other ranges. Its distribution across the rest of Nevada is spotty, with occurrences in the White Mountains and the Sheep, Hot Creek, Monitor, and Silver Peak ranges. The largest stand of bristlecone pine found in Nevada (nearly 18,000 acres) covers the higher parts of the Spring Mountains near Las Vegas.

Living among these high forests are chickadees, nuthatches, sapsuckers and kinglets. Mammals include bighorn sheep and, in some places, yellow-bellied marmots among rocks. White-tailed jackrabbits sometimes frequent the alpine grasslands and open forest areas.

Alpine Zone. Only the highest mountains in Nevada have an alpine zone. Lying beyond the limits of trees, this region is characterized by an extremely short growing season, high winds, high solar radiation, and frequent droughts. Most plants living under these extreme climatic conditions are low growing and mat-like.

Many Nevada ranges have a poorly developed alpine flora. They are simply too dry for development of a true alpine flora. The White Mountains, though higher than the Rubies, have one fourth the number of alpine species primarily because they are too arid to support a diverse flora. Helping support this well developed flora is water. The Rubies are the wettest mountains in the Great Basin and have the most diverse alpine flora with at least 189 species characterized as alpine. Lush alpine meadows are full of genuinely alpine species like swamp laurel, bog orchid, elephant's head, marsh marIgold, bistort and Ross's avens.

But the Rubies are an exception. Most Great Basin Ranges have depauperate alpine flora more similar to that found in the White Mountains. For example, the Toiyabe Range has only 48 species characterized as alpine. Unlike the alpine flora of the Rocky Mountains—derived largely from arctic species that moved south during the Pleistocene Ice Age—many plants found in the alpine zone in most Nevada mountains were originally desert plants that moved upward and adapted to the cold and the limited growing conditions of the alpine world. This zone shows extreme endemism, due to the isolated nature of the habitat.

Ranges with significant alpine areas include the White and Ruby mountains, and the Wassuk, Toiyabe, Toquima, East Humboldt, Grant, Schell Creek and Snake ranges. Other ranges, such as the Spring Mountains near Las Vegas, have relict expanses of alpine terrain as well. The Spring Mountains support the greatest number of alpine endemic species in Nevada.

Animals one might see in the alpine zone include water pipit, rosy finch, golden eagle, pika, yellow-bellied marmot, bighorn sheep, mountain goat (introduced into the Rubies), pocket gopher, deer mouse and golden-mantled ground squirrel.

The title for longevity easily goes to the bristlecone pine, which is known to live almost 5,000 years.

LIVESTOCK GRAZING

To anyone who has spent even a few days in the Nevada mountains, it quickly becomes apparent that of all the human uses, nothing has had as large an ecological impact here, nor as significant an influence on public lands policy and use, as domestic livestock grazing. No book on Nevada's mountains would be complete without discussion of livestock grazing and its effects.

Domestic livestock grazing was introduced into the Great Basin in the 1850s shortly after the first gold and silver discoveries, as a means of feeding hungry mining communities. With the completion of transcontinental railroads, livestock grazing became an export industry, growing cattle and sheep for eastern and west coast markets. By the 1890s, nearly all of Nevada that could even remotely support domestic livestock was being grazed, and by 1918, numbers peaked at 1.2 million sheep and 500,000 cattle. Today, Nevada's vast rangelands are grazed by 93,000 sheep and 383,000 cattle.

Although urban subdivisions and mining activities may be easier to see, no human enterprise affects so many acres over such a huge portion of the state as the livestock industry. But the impacts are often subtle, and they are so pervasive that most people, even ranchers, don't know what the landscape could look like in the absence of livestock.

The most subtle impact has been upon the native vegetation. In a paper on livestock grazing's impact on native vegetation, University of Nevada–Reno professor James Young noted, "The plant communities [of the Great Basin] did not bend or adapt, they shattered."

The evolutionary history of the region's plant communities is one of the reasons the Nevada landscape never supported any large grazing herbivores. No bison roamed the state in recent historical times. Even elk and antelope were uncommon in many areas. The only species that may have been abundant was bighorn sheep.

Above: Cattle graze in the Lehman Creek Campground, Great Basin National Park.

Facing page: An ungrazed, lush, wet meadow on Badger Creek in the Sheldon National Wildlife Refuge gives an indication of what much of Nevada's riparian areas could look like in the absence of livestock grazing.

Large herds of cattle and domestic sheep are not filling some empty niche, but rather are a new ecological influence for which the plant communities have little tolerance. The native plants evolved in the absence of grazing pressure and they don't adapt to cattle or sheep grazing.

Nevada's valleys were always arid and relatively barren. Early travelers often had trouble finding enough feed for the animals in them. But the foothills and mountains were different. For instance, Captain James Simpson crossed Nevada twice in 1859 while locating a wagon road from Utah to the California border. In his journal he noted time and again the generally sparse vegetation encountered in the valleys, and often referred to plentiful grass—in the mountains and foothills. "These valleys…are of great value in furnishing, in great abundance, the small mountain bunchgrass, which has fattening qualities almost, if not quite, equal to oats.…There is quite an abundance of good grass upon the bases of the mountains and in the canyons, and in some places it is found in patches in the valley.…The mules more and more difficult to catch; attribute it to the improved condition, caused by the nutritious properties of the mountain bunchgrass.…The canyons of this mountain abound in pure water and splendid grass."

Sid Tremewan, first supervisor of the Humboldt National Forest in the early 1900s, described the country west of the Jarbidge Mountains in northern Nevada: "Up there on Gold Creek, Walt Martin used to cut his winter hay by mowing the ridges. The native grass was thick enough that all he had to do was find a smooth place.…Prior to the turn of the century, I lived on the Evans Ranch with my uncle. It was wonderful feed country. It was primary a grass range.…All the smoother ridges were covered with bunch grass. There wasn't any sagebrush to speak of, just grass. The creek bottoms from the present highway [Highway 225] to the mountain were continuous narrow meadows. There was no sagebrush in them. The vegetation was mostly redtop and white clover."

While it would be wrong to suggest that sagebrush did not exist in days gone by, those early observations certainly give a different picture of Nevada than one would likely get today. Studies of the vegetation on ungrazed protected areas usually show a mixture of 75 to 90 percent grass, 5 to 15 percent sagebrush, with forbs and other shrubs making up the rest. Today the proportions are frequently reversed, with sagebrush dominating.

These major ecological changes are the result of heavy overgrazing, fire suppression and introduction of cheatgrass, and exotic. Removing grasses by selective grazing has given a competitive advantage to shrubs like sagebrush, and eliminated fine fuels, reducing the occurrence of range fires that periodically burned out sagebrush plants.

Although some rangelands have been under "range management" for more than 80 years, in most cases our rangelands have shown almost no improvement and certainly are far from their potential. According to 1989 figures provided by

riparian zones. In the Elko District of the BLM it was found that 80 percent of the 300 terrestrial species are directly dependent on riparian habitat or use it more than any other habitat. Yet it is in these biologically important areas that cattle

Right: An all too common scene in Nevada are the wide, shallow, cow-trampled streams—banks denuded of vegetation—such as this creek on BLM lands in the Tuscarora Mountains.

Below: Fenceline contrast at Murdock Springs on the Sheldon National Wildlife Refuge. Area outside of fence has been chewed and trampled to bare dirt by cattle.

spend the majority of their time.

Cattle affect riparian areas in a number of ways. By trampling stream banks, they destroy stream channel integrity—turning narrow, deep streams into wide, shallow streams. Ungrazed stream segments nearly always have higher populations of trout and other fish. Furthermore, cattle often will eat stream-side forage down to the ground, reducing hiding cover and nesting habitat for small birds and mammals. One study on

the Bureau of Land Management, only three percent of Nevada BLM rangelands are in "excellent" condition, which represents the potential plant cover a site could support under natural climax-growth conditions. More than 53 percent is in "unsatisfactory" condition, which means it is ecologically trashed.

Far and away, the worst abuses have been to Nevada's very limited, but biologically critical,

BLM lands in northern Nevada found, in ungrazed enclosures, six species of small mammals that were not found in grazed areas. Loss of vegetation also reduces shade, adversely affecting stream temperatures and flows.

Cattle grazing even reduces overall stream flow—in essence, making the desert even more desert-like. In 1978, cattle were removed from a 5.5-mile section of Mahogany Creek in northern

Nevada and, after 10 years, the stream flow had increased by 400 percent, and average stream depth increased by 50 percent.

Despite all the hoopla about range improvement from government agencies like the BLM, according to a 1990 report on western riparian areas by the Environmental Protection Agency, riparian areas were "in the worst shape in history." A 1988 Government Accounting Office report on riparian areas also supported that finding. On one Nevada BLM district, 93 percent and 86 percent of the riparian zones in two separate resource areas were in "poor" to "fair" condition. But such impacts are not limited to BLM lands; in the same report, it was noted that 90 percent of the Austin Ranger District on the Toiyabe National Forest was in a similar condition.

In most cases if the government agencies managing our federal lands do anything about riparian livestock impacts, it is to build more fences, stock ponds, and build pipelines—usually with taxpayer money. Such "solutions" are like building a tall smokestack to dilute pollution: they only spread the impacts over a larger area, and are very costly to implement and maintain. In most cases, termination of livestock grazing altogether would foster far greater ecological improvements as well as prove more cost-effective to taxpayers.

Impacts to riparian areas are not the only problem associated with livestock production. Cattle and sheep grazing uplands eliminate plants that are the only food source for some species of butterflies. Cattle trampling its burrows have adversely affected desert tortoise. Domestic sheep introduce disease that is often fatal to wild bighorns. The list goes on and on. Livestock raising has many more direct impacts to wildlife than any other human action.

In addition to these direct impacts to native plants and animals, there are still other uncounted costs to livestock production. For example, irrigation for livestock forage production is still the largest single reason for dewatering of rivers and groundwater mining in Nevada accounting for 89.6 percent of all water used in the state.

Unfortunately, many endangered species are threatened directly by loss of water to irrigation. The Pyramid Lake cui-ui, an endemic fish known only in that lake, is endangered due to insufficient flows resulting from dewatering the Truckee River where it spawns. The Devil's Hole pupfish was also endangered by ground water pumping that once lowered the water table in its sole habitat—a tiny spring in Ash Meadows National Wildlife Refuge. For the time being, the depletion of the groundwater aquifer has been stabilized. Even entire wildlife refuges are at risk. Demands of irrigators in the Newlands Reclamation Project totally dried up the Winnemucca Lake National Wildlife Refuge, which disappeared in the 1930s—and led to its eventual removal from the refuge system. A similar fate now threatens the Stillwater National Wildlife Refuge.

Domestic livestock are also a major source of water pollution. Barely a spring, stream, or river in Nevada is not fouled by livestock, and given the increasing role and value of recreation in these wildlands, this problem alone is sufficient reason to consider removal of private domesticated animals from much of the public domain. Would we permit humans to pollute these springs and streams with raw sewage? Travelers in Nevada are fined $2,000 for littering roadsides, but it's perfectly legal for cattle to trash entire hillsides and meadows.

One would think that, with the large acreages involved and the tremendous ecological costs, livestock production from Nevada's public lands was essential to the nation. But nothing could be further from the truth. All the millions of acres of public lands in Nevada devoted to livestock production produce only the same amount of beef as tiny Vermont. As we have noted, Nevada agriculture provides less than one percent of the state's jobs; any one of the large casinos in Las Vegas or Reno supports more workers than do all the state's ranches.

Given the natural aridity, fragility and relatively limited productivity of these lands, there is not enough forage, water and space to support both cows and native species. From a national perspective, and these are nationally-owned lands, if we want to protect native biodiversity, watersheds and soils, and maintain ecological processes, there is little room for the additional burden of livestock production in the Great Basin. The nation has plenty of private lands where we can produce beef or mutton, but few places where we can let Lahanton cutthroat trout, Pahrump poolfish, desert tortoises and desert bighorn sheep live. If these animals cannot survive on our public lands, then where can they?

All the millions of acres of public lands in Nevada devoted to livestock production produce only the same amount of beef as tiny Vermont.

CHAPTER THREE

NEVADA HISTORY

People have been living in Nevada for at least 11,000 years, if not longer. The first to arrive stalked mammals such as wooly mammoths.

People have been living in Nevada for at least 11,000 years, if not longer. The first people to arrive were big-game hunters who stalked Ice Age mammals such as wooly mammoths and giant bison. Then, as the climate changed and these large mammals disappeared, people adapted to a more diverse food supply based upon plants and different animals. Different prehistoric native American groups came and went, including a short-term invasion of Anasazi or pueblo-dwelling people in eastern and southern Nevada.

At the time of the first white explorers and settlers, Nevada was inhabited by the southern Paiute or western Shoshone. Compared to other native American groups, these people were extremely poor, earning a meager living on the resources of a stingy landscape. They exploited seasonal food sources from pinyon nuts to fish, and big game like bighorn sheep and antelope as well as smaller animals like lizards, grasshoppers, jackrabbits and rodents. Their housing usually consisted of brush huts.

The native Americans of Nevada could be divided into several major tribal affiliations. The Washoe lived in western Nevada near the base of the Carson Range and around Lake Tahoe. The northern Paiute ranged from southeast Oregon through western Nevada, including from Pyramid Lake to as far south as Walker Lake. The western Shoshone occupied northeast Nevada, while the Mohave and southern Paiutes were found in southern Nevada. As occurred elsewhere, these Indian groups were reduced by disease, poverty and loss of their free-roaming lifestyles once Nevada was invaded by whites. Today their descendants live on a number of small reservations scattered about the state.

The First Whites Explore Nevada

The Great Basin was the last major portion of the United States to be explored and mapped. The first whites actually to enter Nevada were Rocky Mountain fur trappers in pursuit of beaver pelts, who explored much of the western United States. As one might suspect in the state that is more desert-like than any other, beaver trapping was not a particularly lucrative business here.

Nevertheless, the search for pelts spawned a number of exploratory expeditions that put the first geographical names and outlines on the map of what would later be Nevada.

One of the most remarkable, and most widely traveled, of these mountain men was Jedediah Smith. In 1826-1827, he led an expedition from Wyoming south through Utah to the Virgin River, which he followed into Nevada, and he eventually crossed the Mojave Desert into southern California. Leaving most of his party behind in California's Central Valley, Smith, with two companions, floundered through the deep snows of the Sierra in June of 1827 and crossed the desert valleys of central Nevada, suffering from both thirst and hunger. The party followed the Walker River out of the Sierra, skirted the Toiyabe and Toquima ranges, crossed the Monitor and Pancake ranges and rode north over the Schell Creek Range and Snake Range near today's Great Basin National Park and on to the Great Salt Lake, and present-day Wyoming. Despite the hardships, they made the entire trek from California to Wyoming in six weeks.

In 1828-1829, Peter Skene Ogden—for whom Ogden, Utah is named—led a fur trapping expedition into northern Nevada. Ogden worked for the Hudson's Bay Company and, next to Jedediah Smith, probably explored more of the West than any other man of that era. The Hudson's Bay Company controlled the fur trade in Canada, but early on opened trading posts in the Columbia River drainage of Oregon, Washington and Idaho. The Bay sought to keep Americans like Jedediah Smith from expanding west and north and implemented a "scorched earth policy," attempting to trap out all the streams of the Snake River drainage and northern Great Basin. It was up to Ogden to carry out this plan.

In the fall of 1828, Ogden, leading a large brigade of trappers, entered northern Nevada near Denio and worked south to the Quinn River and eventually to the Humboldt River, which he described as lined by willows and full of beaver. Ogden called this river the "Unknown" because he had no idea of where it went or whence it came. It was John Frémont who, several decades later, would bestow the name Humboldt. With winter coming on and little game to sustain a large trapping party through the winter, Ogden took his brigade

Above: Ruins at Delamar ghost town. Gold was discovered in Delamar in 1889, and the town once claimed 1,500 people.

Facing page: Mining ruins at Berlin.

eastward along the Humboldt, crossed the Ruby Mountains and eventually wintered northeast of Great Salt Lake.

In late March of 1829, Ogden broke winter camp and headed west back to the Humboldt, reaching that river on April 11. Ogden and his men trapped the Humboldt westward and took a diversion to the South Fork of the Owyhee north of present-day Tuscarora, before returning to the Humboldt. They followed it to the Humboldt Sink, then retraced their steps to present-day Winnemucca and turned north, skirting the Santa Rosa Range on their homeward journey to Fort Nez Perce in eastern Washington. The next year, Ogden was back, following the Humboldt to its sink and southward to the Walker River and eventually south of Hawthorne, Nevada and to the Gulf of California. This was Ogden's last journey to Nevada.

Genoa Courthouse. Genoa was the first community in Nevada. Established in 1851 by Mormons from Salt Lake City, the town first was named Mormon Station.

Other fur trappers crossed Nevada, including Joseph Walker who, in 1833, followed the Humboldt River across Nevada and made his way over the Sierra, traveling through what is now Yosemite National Park to winter in California. In the spring, his return route took him south of the Sierra via his namesake, Walker Pass, then up the Owens Valley into Nevada. He headed north, crossing the western Nevada river that now bears his name, and eventually reached the Humboldt River and followed it east back to Utah. Walker's journey established that waterway as a feasible land route cutting across Nevada's numerous north-south mountain ranges and dry valleys. Today, Interstate 80 follows the eastern part of that same route.

With the close of the fur trapping era in the late 1830s, the next explorations of Nevada were by military expeditions. One of the first was led by John Frémont guided by the famous mountain man Kit Carson. Entering northwest Nevada in late December 1843, the Frémont party moved south past High Rock Canyon to the Black Rock Desert. They camped at hot springs that they named "Great Boiling Springs" near the present town of Gerlach. In January 1844, they continued south, discovering Pyramid Lake. Frémont worked ever southward, passing the Truckee, Carson and Walker rivers. Then he decided to cross the Sierra, and succeeded, just barely, by way of Carson Pass.

En route, Frémont saw Lake Tahoe, becoming the first white to report this lovely mountain gem.

From California, Frémont circled back across Nevada, following the Old Spanish Trail that passed through the site of Las Vegas and into Utah by way of the Virgin River. Recognizing that none of the rivers in this vast area of interior drainage actually reached the sea, Frémont dubbed the region the Great Basin and the name has stuck to this day.

In 1845, Frémont was back in the West, this time with Joseph Walker as well as Kit Carson as guides. They crossed into Nevada and hit the Humboldt River, which Frémont now named. The party crossed the central part of the state, using Big Smoky Valley by the Toiyabe Range and heading on to Walker Lake. Frémont named both the Walker River and Carson River for his two guides.

Emigrant Trails

Four years before, the first emigrant group to travel what would become known as the California Trail had been the Bidwell-Barteson party. In 1841, they crossed the barren lands north of Great Salt Lake, and entered Nevada near Pilot Peak in today's Elko County. From here they made their way along the Humboldt, losing horses and oxen to fatigue along the way. Eventually, after much hardship including a dreadful snowy crossing of the Sierra, they made their way successfully into the central valley of California.

In 1847, fewer than 500 people trekked overland to California from the East. The next year, the trickle of settlers to California changed to a deluge after gold was discovered in the Sierra foothills. In 1849, an estimated 25,000 emigrants traveled the California Trail across Nevada. The most challenging part of the entire journey was crossing the Forty Mile Desert between Big Meadows (Lovelock) and the waters of the Truckee near present-day Reno. The sinks of the Humboldt and Carson offered almost no forage for weary horses or oxen and no water to drink.

An alternative route, named the Applegate Trail for its first promoter, Jesse Applegate, avoided the hazardous Sierra crossing by going northwest from Lassen Meadows (named for Peter Lassen, along with Mt. Lassen in California) across the Black Rock Desert. After going through High Rock Canyon, the same travelled by Frémont, and on to Goose Lake near the Oregon-California border, the trail turned south into the Sacramento River valley. The trail had its own hazards, including crossing the nearly waterless Black Rock Desert. Nevertheless, thousands of emigrants are said to have traveled this route, assuming that the deep ruts made by the wheels of earlier travelers meant the new route was superior to the main California Trail. In 1850, as many as 50,000 people may have traveled the California Trail across Nevada, leaving behind an estimated 9,000 dead animals and 3,000 wagons scattered along the route.

Mormon Settlers

While most of the people who crossed Nevada were intent on continuing to California, a few actually decided to stay. The first of these settlers were Mormons from Utah. In 1851, a group of 20 Mormons left Salt Lake City to set up a trading post and settlement at the base of the Sierra in the Carson Valley. At "Mormon Station," later to be Genoa, they constructed the first major buildings in Nevada, and traded goods, meat and fresh vegetables to weary emigrants.

At the same time, a slow trickle of non-Mormons began to filter back over the Sierra from California, most of them miners looking for a new bonanza east of the Sierra. But more Mormons continued to make the trek to the Carson Valley, and other small communities sprang up. By 1856, Mormons outnumbered non-Mormons in Nevada.

In 1857, most of the Mormons in the Carson Valley gave up their newly founded homes to hasten back to the Wasatch Front in Utah when fear of a war with the U.S. Army prompted Brigham Young to call his people home. No battle ever resulted, and the U.S. Army and the leaders of the Mormon church averted bloodshed. Nevertheless, the Carson Valley settlements never were recolonized and the Mormon influence in western Nevada waned.

At the same time that Mormons had been building homes in the Carson Valley, Brigham Young sent another contingent to the Las Vegas Valley to build a mission. The mission suffered for a number of reasons and was abandoned in 1858, ending Mormon influence in this part of the state as well.

Today, the only Mormon settlements in the state are in the eastern portion near the Utah border. Baker, near Great Basin National Park, was established by Mormon settlers, as was Panaca, founded in 1864. But, as we shall see, those towns had been founded in Utah Territory, not Nevada.

Miners

Gold had been found in Nevada in limited quantities since 1850. But in 1859, the Comstock Lode, one of the largest silver strikes in the world, brought a rush of prospectors, miners, and speculators to Virginia City, Nevada. The first assays showed the ore was worth more than $3,800 a ton! So many people flooded into Nevada that, by 1861, it was a

territory, and achieved statehood a mere three years later. Virginia City continued to grow in importance and influence, and by 1875 had nearly 20,000 residents.

Miners too late to stake claims at the Comstock Lode spread out across Nevada. New towns sprang up wherever they found pay-dirt. Both Aurora and Unionville were established in 1860. Austin was born in 1862, when silver-bearing ore was discovered. Within weeks, thousands of people had descended on the canyon and the town mushroomed almost overnight. By 1863, Austin was home to more than 10,000 people and became the new county seat. Other discoveries followed: Berlin, Ione, Pioche and Union in 1863, Eureka in 1864, Hamilton and Pahranagat in 1865. The boundaries of Nevada were being mapped out by the locations of mining towns.

The importance of mining cannot be underrated: mining created Nevada. Without it, Nevada may never have become a separate state. Mining spurred both railroad construction and the livestock industry, both important economic factors in the early days.

The Railroad

As towns and commerce spread across Nevada, the nation also was growing as well. The dream was to build a transcontinental railroad that would link California with the Midwest and the east coast. Eastward construction began from Sacramento in 1863, but crossing the Sierra was a difficult task. Not until 1868 did the Central Pacific Railroad reach Truckee Meadows from the west. A railroad station was built there, and around it would grow Reno.

Once across the mountains, the rail crews rapidly laid track across the state. Following the Truckee-Humboldt River route of the fur trappers and emigrants, the crews often laid three miles of tracks a day and, once, eight miles were constructed in a single 24-hour period. In the wake of tracks, towns sprang up: Wadsworth, Lovelock, Winnemucca, Battle Mountain, Carlin, Elko and Wells. The rails reached Promontory, Utah in 1869 and the last spike was driven, linking the nation by railroad from coast to coast.

Expansion

When Nevada became a state in 1864, it did not occupy its current boundaries. Towns including Las Vegas, Ely, Pioche and Boulder City were all outside what was then Nevada. Most of this territory was occupied by Mormons who had established small communities like Panaca, St. Joseph, Moapa, and Overton in western Utah Territory. When gold was discovered at Pahranagat in 1865, Nevada's Con-

The importance of mining cannot be underrated: mining created Nevada.

gressman petitioned the United States government to expand Nevada's borders 50 miles eastward, arguing that a mining town would be served better by Nevada than by Utah. Congress granted Nevada's request and the state was expanded east and south at the expense of Utah and Arizona.

The Livestock Era

The railroad did stimulate another rush, but of a different nature. The livestock industry was established in Nevada to supply the miners with food, but as the mines shut down and towns faded from memory, ranchers were able to turn to national markets by shipping live cattle and sheep on the railroad. Towns like Winnemucca and Elko soon became major livestock shipping centers and supply stations for far-flung livestock operations.

During the 1880s herds grew all around the state, feeding year-round on the native grasslands until the frigid and cold winter of 1889-1890 when temperatures reached 42° below zero in Elko, and the livestock industry was nearly wiped out. But the survivors now adopted the practice of raising hay for winter feed, and began to build their herds once more. Soon livestock numbers exceeded even the previous levels and it became a race between different livestock owners to see whose herd could graze off a piece of land first. By the 1900s most of Nevada's ranges were turning to dust—overgrazed and trampled by what Sierra Club founder John Muir called "hooved locust."

As competition for scarce forage increased, many of the wealthier ranchers hired gunmen to protect what they had come to think of as their property—the vast acreage of public domain lands. Nevertheless, increasing herds threatened the established order of the cattlemen. This was especially true of sheep, which were highly mobile and could move from place to place without the need of a permanent base ranch.

The ranchers were caught in a quandary. They did not want to buy more land, even if they could afford it, because this would necessitate paying taxes on huge acreages of relatively unproductive lands. To eliminate competition, ranchers petitioned the government to establish national forests on summer ranges. These lands were then divided up into allotments among established livestock operations, who then paid a token fee for the privilege of using public forage for their commercial benefit. This effectively eliminated many mobile sheepmen and small cattle operations from getting a cut on the action—precisely the result desired. The allotment system was later adopted for all other public lands including those of the Bureau of Land Management.

Despite the riches associated with Nevada's silver and gold mines, it was copper that ultimately became Nevada's most important metal.

The Twenty-Year Bust and Boom

By 1880, the initial gold and silver rush was over and Nevada sank into a 20-year decline. The state lost one third of its population and by 1900 there were only 42,000 people left in all of Nevada. The only major mineral discovery of the late 1800s was Delamar, discovered in 1890, which eventually produced about $15 million in ore. But this did little to slow Nevada's economic decline.

Then in 1900, new gold discoveries, particularly in south-central Nevada, again spurred growth for the state. Tonopah sprang up in 1900, and was in its heyday by 1905. Production of $250 million worth of gold and silver ore came from Tonopah mines and the town was one of the most prosperous in Nevada for several decades.

As a consequence of the Tonopah discovery, miners again spread out over Nevada looking for new ore deposits. More than a hundred camps sprang up, but only one could match Tonopah for wealth. In 1902, gold was discovered in the dry hills southwest of Tonopah. On this site, the town of Goldfield sprang to life, home to more than 20,000 residents by 1910. Lots sold for $45,000. But by 1920, most of the mines had ceased production. Rhyolite, 75 miles south-southwest of Goldfield in the Amargosa Desert, was founded in a 1904 gold rush and by 1908 more than 8,000 people called this part of the Mojave Desert home.

Despite the riches associated with Nevada's silver and gold mines, it was copper that ultimately became Nevada's most important metal. The center for copper production was Ely in White Pine County. Although copper ore had been known to exist in the Ely area for decades, not until 1900 did interest in copper production develop. The Nevada Consolidated Copper Company was formed in 1904 and by 1906 a railroad line was built to Ely. Two years later, a smelter had been built at McGill north of Ely, and in 1911, Ely was out-producing Goldfield and Tonopah in wealth. Copper was now the number-one mineral in Nevada and remained so for a half century. As of 1960, the Ely mines had produced approximately one third of all the mineral wealth ever taken from Nevada's mountains.

Tourism and Gambling

The mineral booms of the early part of the century were replaced by the gambling boom. Gambling got its start in Nevada with the first miners, and it was rampant in most Nevada mining towns just as it was throughout the West. After the state outlawed it in 1910, gambling simply went underground. In 1931, gambling was officially sanctioned once more so that the state could regulate and tax the operations. Gambling had become big business in Nevada by the end of World War II, and by the 1960s was one of the most lucrative businesses in the world. Hotels and casinos in both Las Vegas and Reno began offering stage shows and other entertainment that pulled in tourists from around the globe.

Government Projects

Although most rural residents might like to think otherwise, it is government, not ranching, mining or other industries, that employs the most people in the hinterlands of Nevada. In most small towns, county, state, and federal jobs all contribute to stabilize the local economies. Without the Bureau of Land Management, Forest Service, Soil Conservation Service and other government jobs, many small Nevada towns would cease to exist.

Big pork-barrel projects like the Hoover Dam on the Colorado River, which employed 5,000 people during the height of its construction, and the Newlands Reclamation Project, which cost millions of dollars and dried up three Nevada lakes and marsh systems to irrigate the desert near Fallon, are both examples of government-subsidized projects that have had local economic, if not environmental, benefits.

The military is another big employer in the state. The army chose Hawthorne in 1930 as a site for an ammunition depot and, during World War II, more than 13,000 people were living in the town—most working for the military or serving its personnel. But government is even responsible for many urban jobs as well. Nellis Air Force Base and the Nevada Test Site, both near Las Vegas, employ thousands of people.

The New Mining Boom

In the 1980s Nevada experienced its third major gold rush boom and is now host to anout 60 percent of all U.S. gold production. Using new techniques like cyanide heap-leaching, even microscopic traces of gold could be profitably recovered by strip-mining the ore and then washing it in a weak solution of cyanide. More than 603,587 mining claims have been staked on public lands in the state. By the early 1990s more than 120 mines were operating in Nevada, many reworking old mining areas including abandoned talus piles. Towns like Tuscarora, Midas, Rhyolite, Manhattan, and others that once had busted are now repopulated and experiencing a resurgence of population and investment interest. Mining in Nevada is now a $2-billion-a-year industry. The Carlin Trend near Carlin may be the largest gold mining operation in the world, stretching nearly 40 miles across northern Nevada.

Major problems exist, though. Due to the archaic Mining Law of 1872, federal agencies don't have the authority to simply say no. If an economically valuable mineral deposit exists, it can be mined regardless of what other public resources may be compromised or lost. In addition, concerns have arisen about proper reclamation and the scars mining can leave upon the landscape. Furthermore, mining booms bring major problems to rural communities such as housing shortages and over-crowded schools, matched by equally empty houses and schools after the mines close. There is no free lunch.

The New Frontier

Tourism is actually Nevada's biggest industry and it continues to grow. But not everyone moving to Nevada is a tourist. Many come to live and work because they find Nevada's natural environment a major attraction. It has a dry, sunny climate, excellent transportation links and a growing importance as an outdoor recreation paradise. There are few other places in the United States where one could be windsurfing in 85° weather on Lake Mead and then going downhill skiing that afternoon. Yet, these are the kinds of options available to most Nevadans. Developments like Lake Mead National Recreation Area provide for year-round boating, sailing, swimming and fishing, while resorts and ski areas make Lake Tahoe a winter haven. In addition to these more developed attractions, Nevada has millions of acres of deserts, mountains, and basins that are publicly owned and accessible to everyone.

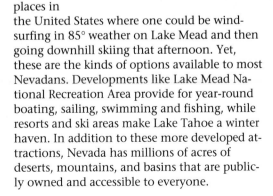

Above: Ruins at the old mining town of Belmont in the Toquima Range.
Top: *The partial ghost town of Tuscarora is in the Tuscarora Mountains.*

CHAPTER FOUR

WESTERN NEVADA

Due to its proximity to the main Sierran crest, the Carson Range has the most diverse tree and wildlife species encountered in Nevada.

Western Nevada is the smallest region of the state, running from Reno and the Truckee River to Fallon, then south to Walker Lake and continuing on to the Fish Lake Valley east of the White Mountains to an intersection with the California border. Within this region is Nevada's outlier of the Sierra Nevada, the Carson Range, plus other major and more typical Great Basin ranges including the Wassuk, Pine Nut, Virginia, Excelsior, Sweetwater, and White mountains. Here rises Nevada's highest peak, 13,140-foot Boundary Peak. The Lahontan Trough lowlands separate these peaks, largely granitic in composition, from ranges farther east.

Reno and Carson City are the population centers with nearly a quarter of Nevada's population located in the region as defined, which includes towns like Fallon and Hawthorne on its edges.

The best known mountain range in this part of Nevada, and perhaps the best known statewide because of its location on the eastern shore of Lake Tahoe, is the Carson Range. More than 50 miles long, with its highest summit, Freel Peak, at 10,881 feet, the Carson Range is named for guide Kit Carson who crossed it with John Frémont in 1844.

The Carson Range is part of the huge Sierra Nevada mountain range that lies mostly in California. Roughly 50 to 100 miles wide and more than 400 miles long, the Sierra is one of the larger granitic mountain masses in North America. The western slope is long and gentle, while the eastern slope is steep and abrupt.

In the region just west of Carson City, a chunk of this immense Sierran block broke away from the main crest to form the Carson Range, with Lake Tahoe occupying the valley that dropped between the two uplifted mountains.

The main Sierran crest blocks the westward movement of moisture-laden air so that the west shore of Lake Tahoe in California receives an average of 60 inches of precipitation a year, while the Carson Range, lying in the rainshadow, gets only 30 inches. Yet, as dramatic as that difference in annual precipitation may be, by the time you get to the Carson Valley below the Carson Range crest, precipitation has dropped to 5 inches or less.

Due to its proximity to the main Sierran crest, the Carson Range has the most diverse tree and wildlife species encountered in Nevada. Here one will find 11 wildlife species found nowhere else in the state, including black bear, red squirrel, northern flying squirrel, snowshoe hare, marten, lodgepole chipmunk, long-eared chipmunk, Townsend's chipmunk, mountain pocket gopher, Trowbridge's shrew and mountain beaver. Trees are equally as diverse and abundant, including species rare or absent farther east in Nevada's Great Basin ranges, like lodgepole pine, western white pine, Jeffrey pine, incense cedar, mountain hemlock, red fir, sugar pine, and a species found nowhere else in the Silver State—the Washoe pine. Most of the Carson Range's fine forests are second-growth, the virgin timber having been cut to build the mines and houses in Virginia City during its heyday.

Most of the Carson Range is managed as part of the Toiyabe National Forest. The Mount Rose area, just a short drive from Reno, is protected within the 28,000-acre Mount Rose Wilderness Area.

Virginia Mountains

Directly across the Truckee Meadows from the Mount Rose portion of the Carson Range lies the Virginia Mountains. Unlike many Nevada mountain ranges, the Virginias trend more northeast to southwest, separating the Truckee and Carson rivers. This is rolling country, not particularly rugged, with Mt. Davidson, the highest peak, a mere 7,864 feet in elevation.

The Virginia Mountains are best known for the Comstock Lode—one of the richest silver deposits in the world. Strung out on a slope of Mt. Davidson lies Nevada's most enduring mining town, Virginia City, once one of its most bawdy. Just a few years after the great California gold rush in 1849, disgruntled miners began to wander over the Sierra into Nevada looking for new pay dirt. Limited quantities of placer gold were found in the Carson Valley—enough to keep a couple hundred miners in the area looking for more. In 1859,

Facing page: Fir and pine frame Lake Tahoe and the Carson Range.

they found it—a quartzite lode that contained some promising gold-bearing ore. When the ore was assayed in California, it turned out to have a lot of gold, but even more silver, an incredible $3,000 per ton. The following spring, more than 10,000 people descended on the slopes of Mt. Davidson and Virginia City was born. Several booms and busts followed, even a fire in 1875 that destroyed much of the downtown, but they didn't discourage the hopeful. By 1876, Virginia City had 23,000 citizens, then half of Nevada's population. But a few years later the ore bodies finally played out and Virginia City began its inevitable decline. Today the community is back in the mining business, but this time mining mostly tourists' pocketbooks, rather than ore in the ground.

Pine Nut Mountains

To the south of the Virginia Mountains across the Carson River and directly east of Minden is the rolling Pine Nut Mountains. Named for the pinyon tree and its edible nut, this mountain uplift reaches 9,450 feet on the top of Mount Siegel. For most of its 40 miles, it stays at or near 9,000 feet.

These mountains are geologically complex, with both sedimentary and volcanic outcrops. Granitic intrusives make up a great deal of the range's rocks. Silver, lead and zinc were all mined in the area, along with copper and molybdenum. Numerous hot springs mark the fault zone along the eastern flank of the range.

Compared to the Carson Range just across the valley, the vegetation here is not very diverse. It includes black cottonwood, chokecherry, aspen, wild rose, and of course, pinyon woodland. Douglas squirrels, generally restricted to the Sierran block, are found in this range. A small Bureau of Land Management wilderness study area, Burbank Canyons, lies along the southern edge of the range.

Wassuk Range

Forming a dramatic backdrop for the western shore of Walker Lake near Hawthorne is the predominantly granitic mass of the Wassuk Range. Here are the easternmost reaches of the Sierran granite. Rising to 11,239 feet in elevation, Mt. Grant towers more than 7,200 feet above the waters of the lake. (This is about 200 feet more relief than that of the Grand Teton rising above Jackson Hole.) The range stretches south 65 miles from the Walker River on the north to the Anchorite Hills in the south. Walker Lake and the river are named for mountain man Joseph Walker who, with a party of 60 trappers, passed this way in 1833 en route to California.

Left: Mount Rose in the Mount Rose Wilderness, which lies in Reno's backyard.
Above: Boundary Peak in the White Mountains, at 13,140 feet, is Nevada's highest peak. It's seen here from Fish Lake Valley.

Facing page: A quiet morning in Virginia City, site of the Comstock Lode, one of the richest silver deposits ever discovered.

The Wassuk Range, like many ranges in western Nevada, is rotated somewhat from the north-south pattern so typical of the rest of the Great Basin. The cause of this rotation is a fault system somewhat like the famous San Andreas Fault in California, and more or less parallel with it, called the Walker Lane. Mountains along this fault are moving southeastward relative to California, and are being twisted away from their otherwise north-south orientation as a consequence.

The Carson Range, a sub-range of the Sierra Nevada Mountains of California, rises abruptly along a fault scarp near Minden.

Due to its proximity to the Sierra, the Wassuk Range is home to several tree species not found farther east in Nevada, including western white pine and Jeffrey pine. But perhaps the most interesting feature of the Wassuk Range is the lack of livestock grazing. A good portion of the range, including the higher elevations around Mount Grant, are part of the Hawthorne Army Ammunition Depot, where livestock grazing has been prohibited for over 60 years. Botanists who have had the opportunity to see this ungrazed rangeland rave about its beauty, diversity of species, and excellent condition of the grasses. A small herd of 50 desert bighorns roam the range.

Excelsior Mountains

To the south of Hawthorne, partially in California, are the jumbled ridges and canyons of the Excelsior Mountains, another range in the Walker Lane that has been rotated into an east-west alignment. Composed primarily of Sierran granitic rocks, this 37-mile-long range reaches its high point on 8,805-foot Moho Mountain. The western edge of the range is bounded by Mono Lake.

Covered with dense pinyon forests (but no juniper), the area is seldom grazed by domestic livestock, and as a consequence has rich native grasslands and wildflower meadows. A small herd of antelope occasionally venture into this area, and a resident herd of fewer than 50 desert bighorn sheep call these granitic ridges home.

Managed by both the BLM and Forest Service, a minimum of 125,000 acres of the Toiyabe National Forest lands in Nevada are road-less and were proposed as wilderness by the Friends of Nevada Wilderness for inclusion in the 1989 Nevada Wilderness bill. Unfortunately this area was left out of the legislation.

White Mountains

The highest peak in Nevada is almost in California. Boundary Peak, at 13,140 feet, is the top of the Silver State, and lies less than a mile from the Golden State. Although the granitic summit of Boundary Peak is the highest point in the White Mountains within Nevada, even higher peaks are found farther south in the California portion of the range, with the 14,246-foot summit of White Mountain Peak, the apex of the range. Compared to the rugged glaciated wall of the Sierra across the Owens Valley, the White Mountains are relatively rounded and smooth. But when viewed from Fish Lake Valley, the east side of the snow-covered White Mountains look almost Himalaya-like in size and scale.

Lying in the rainshadow of the Sierra Nevada wall, the White Mountains get barely enough moisture to sustain tree growth. The Bancroft Laboratory alpine research facility, at 12,470 feet on the California side of the range, gets only 15 inches of precipitation a year! This dryness makes the White Mountains prime bristlecone pine country. Scattered along the crest of the range are groves of some of the oldest trees in North America, some still living after 4,000 years. But the lack of water means fewer ecological niches for plants and, as a consequence, the White Mountains are home to only 48 alpine plants, considerably fewer than the 189 recorded for the wetter Ruby Mountains near Elko.

This area is part of the transition zone where the Mojave Desert pushes farthest north. At the lowest elevations in Fish Lake Valley, along the east slope of the White Mountains, grow cholla and blackbrush as well as sagebrush and rabbitbrush. The slopes of the White Mountains are dominated by forests of pinyon pine and mountain mahogany with sagebrush growing up to 12,000 feet in elevation. Water is relatively abundant in the numerous canyons that cut the eastern flank of the range. Wildlife includes ring-tail cat, mountain lion, bighorn sheep, mule deer, yellow-bellied marmot, Nuttall's cottontail, Inyo shrew, and pika.

Ten thousand acres around Boundary Peak on the Toiyabe National Forest have been protected as the Boundary Peak Wilderness Area.

LAKE TAHOE

The border between California and Nevada splits Lake Tahoe in half, with 29 of its 72 miles of shoreline in Nevada. The lake, sitting at 6,230 feet above sea level, is the largest mountain lake in the world—22 miles long by 12 miles wide—surrounded by mountains that rise over 10,000 feet. Its greatest depth, 1,645 feet, makes Lake Tahoe the tenth deepest lake in the world and third deepest in North America. The bottom of the lake, at 4,580 feet, is actually 92 feet lower in elevation than Carson City. Because of its great depth, the lake has never frozen, so remains a blue jewel framed by white mountains even in winter.

Lake Tahoe is cradled by two immense fault blocks of the Sierra Nevada granitic block, with the eastern margin in Nevada named the Carson Range and the more western, California, block the main crest of the Sierra Nevada. The block between these uplifted mountain ranges slid downward, forming the Lake Tahoe basin. After the faulting, lava from a volcano dammed the Truckee River, backing up water that created the lake. As the lake filled, it eventually carved an outlet through the lava dam, creating the present outlet for the Truckee River. During the last Ice Age, huge glaciers formed on the Sierra side of the lake and flowed down tributary canyons, carving U-shaped valleys and depositing moraines and other glacial debris. Emerald Bay, on the California side, is nearly enclosed by remnants of glacial moraine.

For generations, the Washoe Indians spent summers on the shore of Lake Tahoe fishing, and no doubt enjoying the lake and the scenery as today's visitors do. In 1844, John Frémont, the "pathfinder," followed the Truckee River upstream into the Sierra and recorded seeing the lake.

In the late 1800s Tahoe was discovered both as a resort and as a place for timber production. Most of the forestlands were logged off. The forests we see here today are almost all second growth. The selective harvest took mainly pines, leaving behind less valuable fir, which is more susceptible to disease and drought—making the Tahoe Basin a major fire hazard today.

The first railroad reached the basin in 1900, easing access and spurring the lake's development as a summer retreat. The wealthy met here to hobnob with friends from San Francisco and Virginia City. Their opulent homes can be viewed at Tallac Historic Site on the south shore.

Casinos, built in the 1940s, and the 1960 Squaw Valley Olympics assured the area its status as a major year-round resort area. Spawning

developments began to change the character of the lake basin forever.

Fortunately for most visitors and residents alike, most (85 percent) of the Tahoe Basin is state or federally owned, which prevents total destruction of the goose that laid the golden egg, by restricting development to a small percentage of the basin. Three wilderness areas—Desolation and Granite Chief in California and Mount Rose in Nevada—ring the lake. Much of the Nevada shoreline is protected in Lake Tahoe State Park.

Because of its great depth, the lake has never frozen, so remains a blue jewel framed by white mountains even in winter.

Granitic boulders along the shore of Lake Tahoe, Toiyabe National Forest. Reaching a depth of 1,645 feet, Tahoe is one of the ten deepest lakes in the world.

NORTHWEST NEVADA

This is not a region of great elevation—the highest point, Duffer Peak of the Pine Forest Range, reaches only 9,458 feet.

Northwest Nevada is as much deserts and mesas as it is mountains. Overall, this is not a region of great elevation—the highest point, Duffer Peak of the Pine Forest Range, reaches only 9,458 feet. Although most mountains are no more than 7,000 to 8,000 feet in elevation, some of the valleys are only 4,000 feet or so above sea level, so total relief can still be great. Perhaps due to their relative lack of elevation, most ranges are nearly devoid of trees, except for the ever-present juniper at lower elevations and aspen in the middle elevations or around seeps. The lowest elevations have shadscale and saltbush desert vegetation, with sagebrush-grassland running all the way to the summits of the peaks.

This region takes in all the mountains north of Interstate 80 and the Humboldt River, and west of Highway 95 in the upper Quinn River Valley to the California and Oregon borders. The only substantial town in the area is Gerlach, and even this is home to not more than a few hundred souls. Both Lovelock and Winnemucca are located to the southeast.

Trinity, Truckee, Nightingale, Selenite Ranges

Paralleling the Humboldt River is the Trinity Range, nearly 60 miles long but overall a low range. The highest peak is 7,337-foot Trinity Peak west of Lovelock. These mountains are made up of a variety of rock types, from granite outcrops to basalts and slates. The granite forms serrated ridges in some parts of the range. Since the first white settlers came into the region, and probably for a long time before that, the Humboldt River corridor was a major passageway across Nevada's waterless valleys. It became the chosen route for railroads and, later, highways. Much land ownership consists of "checkerboard" (alternating) railroad sections, a government giveaway to the transcontinental railroads as an incentive for constructing tracks across the West.

Farther west over low rolling hills and uplands, are the Truckee, Nightingale and Selenite ranges. The Truckee is composed of Tertiary volcanics, while the Nightingale and Selenite ranges, both very narrow, are primarily granites. The highest point in the Nightingale Mountains is below 7,000 feet, while the Selenite rises to 8,237 feet at Kumiva Peak. The Selenite Range is particularly serrated and knife-like. It gets its name from the mineral selenite, a form of gypsum. All three ranges are dominated by desert shrubs such as sagebrush, winterfat, shadscale, and desert peach. Higher elevations have very limited juniper, but several aspen groves are found in the Selenite Range.

To the east of the Nightingale Range lies the dried-up lake bed of Winnemucca Lake—a relict of Lake Lahontan—once a national wildlife refuge. But diverting water from the Truckee and Carson rivers for agricultural use led to the eventual loss of the lake and the entire wildlife refuge.

Fox Range

West of the Selenite Range and nearly surrounded by the Smoke Creek Desert is the 26-mile-long Fox Range, whose crown is the granitic 7,608-foot Pah-Rum Peak. The western side has some steep canyons and bowl-like basins, while the eastern side has a gentler slope. Vegetation is sparse, mostly desert shrub, with a few scattered junipers. In 1843-1844, John Frémont and guide Kit Carson skirted the eastern edge of this range during their first exploration of Nevada. Later, around the turn of the 20th century, gold, silver, and tungsten were mined in Cottonwood, Wild Horse, and Rodeo canyons, but production never was extensive.

In a demonstration of the livestock industry's influence on land use, a 1987 BLM report stated that 98 percent of the range within the Fox Range was considered to be in "fair" to "poor" condition. In other words, the land was ecologically devastated. Yet not only was grazing allowed to continue, but also officials anticipated no planned reductions or shortening of season. Similar reports exist for nearly all BLM grazing allotments in this part of the state.

Facing page: *Colorful volcanic rock outcrops give the Calico Mountains their name.*

Pyramid Lake

Flanking Pyramid Lake on the west and southwest are the Virginia Mountains and Pah Rah Range, respectively, with Mullen

Above: Reeds and sedges in the Black Rock Desert near Gerlach, with the Granite Range beyond.
Right: Indian ricegrass along Highway 447. The Lake Range forms the skyline.

Facing page: Desert peach in bloom; looking toward Big Mouth Canyon in the Pah Rah Range.

Pass separating the two. In the Virginia Mountains, standing nearly 5,000 feet above Pyramid Lake, is 8,722-foot Tule Peak, while Virginia Peak in the Pah Rah Range rises to 8,367 feet. Both ranges are geologically similar, composed primarily of volcanic rocks such as basalts, rhyolite and andesites extruded during the last 20 million years.

Pyramid Lake, which lies at the base of these mountains, is a living vestige of 200-by-175 mile glacial Lake Lahontan. Since the last Ice Age, a warming climate has evaporated much of the old glacial lake and Pyramid is all that's left behind. The lake was named by John Frémont in 1844, when his party passed a shoreline rock formation that reminded him of the pyramid of Cheops.

Near the current location of the town of Nixon, Frémont visited an Indian village where he was treated to a feast of trout. Giant fish up to 35 pounds swam up the Truckee River from the lake and their numbers sustained the Indians for generations. But with the construction of the Newlands Reclamation Project in 1905, water was gradually diverted from the Truckee River to hay fields, Pyramid Lake dropped 100 feet, and the spawning run was destroyed. Reintroduced in 1975, large cutthroat trout again populate the lake. But water diversion still threatens another Pyramid Lake fish, the cui-ui, a relict of the Ice Age and a kind of sucker found nowhere else in the world. This species also is endangered, because lack of water prevents it from reaching the river where they spawn.

Granite Range, Calico Mountains

As you approach Gerlach from the south on Highway 447, the steep face of the Granite Range looms ahead like the prow of a boat. This "prow" splits the Black Rock Desert into two halves, the western portion known as the Smoke Creek Desert. Both Black Rock and Smoke Creek are playas, or dried lake beds. During the Ice Age, most of the valleys in northwest Nevada were under the waters of Lake Lahontan, and the deserts are physical reminders of this.

In December 1843, John Frémont camped below the Granite Mountains at "Great Boiling Springs," and indeed, the springs do boil as they bubble up out of the ground. Granite Peak, 9,611 feet in elevation, is the highest mountain, rising more than a mile above the Black Rock Desert.

West of Gerlach and north of the Smoke Creek Desert are the Buffalo Hills, a volcanic plateau with steep escarpments typical of the

rest of northwest Nevada. Much of the area is a BLM wilderness study unit of more than 142,000 acres. Poodle Mountain, only 6,832 feet in elevation, was once a volcanic vent. From this vent, basaltic lava flowed, covering much of the area.

terminus of the range, gives the surrounding desert its name. The Black Rock Range high point is 8,798-foot Mt. Lander. Once again John Frémont enters the story—he described the range's namesake during his 1844 expedition: "We passed the rocky cape, a jagged,

Sunrise over the Smoke Creek Desert, a playa once filled with the waters of glacial Lake Lahontan.

Northeast of the Granite Range lie the Calico Mountains, named for the brightly colored basalt and andesite volcanic rocks that make up the range. At 8,491 feet, Donnelly Peak forms the apex of the range. Petrified wood is found in Petrified Canyon, and Donnelly Creek Canyon on the eastern side of the range holds lovely riparian vegetation. The Applegate-Lassen Trail passed the eastern border of the unit. Today, the road to Soldier Meadows basically follows the trail route.

Black Rock Range, Jackson Mountains

Across from the Calicos lies the 50-mile-long Black Rock Range. A prominent, black, volcano-looking plug, marking the southern

broken point, bare and torn." But it was emigrants using the Applegate-Lassen Trail who bestowed the name Black Rock on the prominent rock outcrop near the range's southern terminus. This outcrop marked the location of the welcome hot springs that lie near the mountain's base.

Two BLM wilderness study areas—one of 30,000 acres and the other of 57,000—encompass two different parts of the Black Rock Range, including Pahute Peak, one of the highest summits in the range. In the northern portion of the range Mahogany Creek is a spawning area for Lahontan cutthroat trout, a threatened species. Geodes, petrified wood, and opals have all been found here.

Farther east across the white expanse of the Black Rock Desert are the Jackson Mountains, a 46-mile-long range. Its steep western escarpment rises nearly 5,000 feet to the top of turreted, knife-edged, 8,923-foot King Lear Peak, the highest peak in the range.

This largely volcanic range is a remnant of an island arc or an off-shore island group that was driven by plate tectonic motion up against what was then the western edge of the North American continent. Mineral exploration has turned up copper, lead, zinc, silver and iron here.

The western flank of the range is riddled with rugged, deep canyons like Mike O'Brien, New Year's, Deer Creek, Mary Sloan, Alaska, Bliss, and McGill that provide access to the mountains. A few of the canyons have water, McGill being the most popular with hikers. Here one finds cottonwood trees, wildflowers, and shrubs like red osier dogwood, chokecherry and snowberry. Juniper and aspen are the only other tree species. Two BLM wilderness study areas, North Jackson and South Jackson, are located in the range.

Bordering the Black Rock Range on the east and west of the Jackson Mountains is the Black Rock Desert BLM wilderness study area, more than 300,000 acres in size and the second largest WSA in the lower 48 states. The significance of the area was suggested by the BLM, which noted that the Black Rock is one of the last virtually undeveloped desert valley floors in the West. The dry lake bed, as Rose Strickland of the Sierra Club has pointed out, is one of the few basins within the Basin and Range province proposed for protection in a natural state. If for no other reason, this area warrants wilderness designation.

Pine Forest Range

At the northern edge of the Black Rock Desert lies the Pine Forest Range, another largely granitic range with a Sierra-like feel to it. Duffer Peak, at 9,428 feet, is the highest summit in the range, as well as in northwest Nevada. These mountains were high enough to support glaciers during the last Ice Age, and Pine Forest is the only range in northwest Nevada with such glacial features as moraines, cirques and the glacially carved lake basin occupied by Blue Lakes. The range has flowery meadows and scenic granitic outcrops. Like other ranges in the region, its isolation has prevented colonization by many tree species and the only conifer is whitebark pine, although aspen is also abundant. Two small BLM wilderness study areas surround the Blue Lakes area.

Two other minor mountain ranges lie east of Denio: the 40-mile-long Bilk Creek Mountains and the Trout Creek-Montana Mountains which are across the Kings River Valley farther east. The highest elevations in any of these ranges is approximately 8,500 feet. Despite their height, these are relatively gentle mountains, more rolling than rugged. One exception is the area around Disaster Peak in the Trout Creeks, which has a steep escarpment visible for miles, as well as the collapsed rim of the McDermit Caldera where outcrops of granite occur within an area of predominantly volcanic rock.

Sheldon National Wildlife Refuge

Going west from Denio to the California border, one finds mostly upland plateau country. A good portion of Nevada's northwest corner is encompassed by the Sheldon National Wildlife Refuge—one of the largest wildlife refuges in the lower 48 states. The refuge, set aside to protect antelope, is also home to bighorn sheep, Lahontan cutthroat, and the Sheldon tui chub, also a threatened species. The area is mostly rolling sagebrush country with scattered aspen and juniper. Virgin Creek cuts a dramatic gorge through Thousand Springs Mountain, one of eight wilderness study areas on the refuge. Bighorn sheep were recently introduced into this area.

Unfortunately, this area is like most of Nevada, supporting more cows than anything else—much to the detriment of the antelope, for which it was originally set aside. Livestock have devastated the refuge, causing extensive destruction of riparian areas, degrading wet meadows, accelerating arroyo-cutting, and triggering significant changes in plant communities. Fortunately, the present refuge manager is attempting to reverse some of the trends.

Snow amidst rabbitbrush on the volcanic plateaus that make up northwest Nevada, seen here on the Sheldon National Wildlife Refuge.

NORTHEAST NEVADA

Large stands of aspen, and some widely scattered stands of limber pine near the crest, are the only tree species found in the Santa Rosa Range.

I n a state that is almost all mountains, northeast Nevada actually has large areas without mountains at all, and even the ranges that are here are not the highest or the longest. But that should not dissuade people from investigating this part of the state, for this region has some gems of its own. As defined, northeast Nevada takes in everything east of Highway 95 and north of Interstate 80 up to the Oregon and Idaho borders on the north and the Utah border on the east. Within this area are such lovely mountain ranges as the Santa Rosa, Jarbidge, Independence, and the small, but prominent, Pilot Range.

Santa Rosa Range, Owyhee Desert

Starting on the west and moving east, the first major mountain uplift is the Santa Rosa Range which is directly east of Highway 95, the road that runs between Winnemucca and McDermitt. The range has a central crest that runs more or less north-south for 50 miles up to the Oregon border with the highest eminence, Granite Peak, rising more than 5,500 feet above the surrounding lowlands to 9,732 feet. As the name Granite Peak implies, the range has large outcrops of granite, but shattered, spired, volcanic rocks also appear in the northern end of these mountains.

Large stands of aspen, and some widely scattered stands of limber pine near the crest, represent the only tree species found in the Santa Rosa Range. As a consequence, sagebrush is found all the way to the crest of the range. Numerous perennial streams flow off the mountains into the nearby thirsty valleys.

The first whites into the region were trappers. Peter Skene Ogden and his party trapped the Quinn River to the west of the range in 1829. The next record dates from 1863 when several prospectors from Star City on the Humboldt River were crossing the Santa Rosa Range on an exploratory expedition. They were so impressed with the landscape at the foot of the Santa Rosas that they exclaimed: "What a paradise!" and immediately claimed homesteads in the beautiful valley. That fall nearly 250 tons of Paradise Valley wild hay was cut and transported to Star City for sale. Paradise City was established in 1866 and by 1881 had 100 residents. According to early reports, the Santa Rosa Range had "wonderful Idaho fescue and bluebunch wheatgrass ranges" and, by 1880, ranching was well established in the range.

As occurred throughout Nevada, by the turn of the 20th century, overgrazing destroyed the "wonderful" ranges. In 1911, presidential order established the Santa Rosa National Forest to regulate grazing. Since then, administration for the range has been shuffled back and forth between the Humboldt and Toiyabe national forests and today, the Santa Rosa Ranger District is part of the Humboldt National Forest. In 1989, 31,000 acres in the range were officially designated wilderness.

Regulation of domestic livestock here by the Forest Service has largely been ineffective, and not in the long-term public interest. The rangelands of the Santa Rosa Range are some of the most trampled and eroded areas I have seen on any forest lands in Nevada.

Directly east from the Santa Rosa is the Owyhee Desert, a rolling plateau of sagebrush-covered basalt flows and deeply dissected river canyons. It is one of the most extensive non-mountainous areas in the entire state of Nevada.

South of the desert and north of the Humboldt River near Golconda lie the Osgood Mountains. A number of recent heap-leach mining operations occur in this range, whose highest summit is 8,678-foot Adam Peak.

To the east across the Kelley Creek Valley lie the Owyhee Bluffs and the Snowstorm Mountains—a western outlier of the main ridgeline. The Owyhee Bluffs mark the southern boundary of the Owyhee Desert. Unlike most of the Nevada uplands, this ridge runs 35 miles southwest to northeast and connects to the Tuscarora Mountains. A cliff-like escarpment marks the southern bounds of the bluffs, giving rise to their name. The old gold mining of town of Midas is located here,

Facing page:
Whitebark pine at McAfee Peak in the Independence Mountains.

and several other recent gold mining ventures are scattered in the surrounding mountains.

Lahontan cutthroat trout are found in the Little Humboldt River, which runs off the Snowstorm Mountains. Antelope live throughout the Owyhee Desert country and range up into the northern flanks of the Owyhee Bluffs. In addition, California bighorn sheep were reintroduced into the area in 1988.

Tuscarora Mountains

The next significant uplands are the Tuscarora Mountains, a rather indistinct limestone range nearly 70 miles long and as much as 20 miles wide. The highest peak is Beaver Peak, 8,786 feet high.

In the northern and eastern slopes of the Tuscarora Mountains are the headwaters of the South Fork of the Owyhee River. In the days before dams on the Columbia and Owyhee rivers blocked human passage, livestock grazing ruined riparian areas, and irrigation diversion dried up tributary streams, the South Fork saw salmon runs. Early settlers, regularly catching 30-pound fish, actually speared them with pitchforks and took salmon out by the wagon load. Like other natural resources, Owyhee salmon are only a faded memory and just one part of Nevada's biological heritage that has been lost forever.

The range derives its name from the town of Tuscarora, which sprang up in 1867 when gold was discovered in the mountains. The town faded after the gold ran out, but recently, new heap-leach mining operations have begun to eat away at the mountains and town both.

Lahontan cutthroat trout are found in the Little Humboldt River, which runs off the Snowstorm Mountains.

Independence Mountains

Across the Independence Valley lie the Independence Mountains. McAffee Peak, at 10,439 feet, is the highest summit in this 70-mile-long range. The northern portion has several other peaks above 10,000 feet and was high enough to experience limited glaciation during the last Ice Age. Glacial cirques and other ice-carved features give it a rugged, alpine appearance. Subalpine fir, a Rocky Mountain species, grows here, along with whitebark pine and aspen. The North Fork of the Humboldt River supports native Humboldt cutthroat trout, a rare species.

When the Independence National Forest (now part of the Humboldt National Forest) was established in 1908, one of the immediate problems was "sheep mining." Individuals filed placer mining claims to springs, waterholes and creeks, then charged sheepherders for watering privileges. The Forest Service stepped in and by not recognizing any claims that failed to show mineral value, put an end to this practice.

Today, the Independence Mining Company has a huge open-pit strip mine along the headwaters of the North Fork of the Humboldt, and mining exploration roads scar a considerable amount of the range. Other mining operations also occur in this range, particularly near California Mountain.

Jarbidge Mountains

East of the Independence Range is a hummocky uplands drained by the Jarbidge, Bruneau and Owyhee rivers. The most westerly portion is sometimes called the Mahogany Mountains, then east are the Copper Mountains, and next the Jarbidge Mountains. The majority of the exposed rock is volcanic in nature, though some areas hold outcrops of granite.

When the first national forests were established in northeast Nevada in 1908, 560,000 sheep grazed in the Independence, Gold Creek and Jarbidge ranger districts. Within a year, the Forest Service cut sheep numbers by more than 200,000 animals. Despite the reductions, this country still is overgrazed by both sheep and cattle, riparian areas are trampled, soils are eroding from livestock use, and the abundant

Above: *Lush growth in ungrazed riparian area of the Upper Mary's River, Jarbidge Mountains Wilderness, Jarbidge Mountains.*

Facing page: *Granite outcrop in the Granite Mountains along the headwaters of the Salmon Falls River.*

Above: *Sunset on the crest of the Jarbidge Mountains, as seen from Bear Creek Summit.*

Facing page: *Trail riding in the Jarbidge Wilderness Area.* LARRY PROSOR PHOTO

grass that once covered these mountains is but a memory. One exception is the headwaters of the West Fork of the Mary's River, where grazing has been prohibited for 30 years. Here riparian meadows are beginning to show some signs of recovery from nearly the 80 years of overgrazing. The streamside meadows are lush and thick, stream channels narrow, and wildflowers abundant. Lahontan cutthroat trout are found in the drainage.

The highest parts of these uplands are known as the Jarbidge Mountains. A crest of high peaks, eight of them more than 10,000 feet in elevation, lies at the headwaters of the Jarbidge River. The highest is Matterhorn, its summit 10,839 feet. In the early days, miners who lived in the area thought that the many glaciated cirque basins were formed by volcanic eruptions, and called this range the Crater Range. A number of glacial lakes and tarns are scattered around these high peaks, and the area is protected as part of the 113,200-acre Jarbidge Wilderness Area.

Elk are found on the eastern side of the Jarbidge Mountains adjacent to the O'neil Basin. Another group of elk were recently established by the Forest Service in the Bruneau River headwaters.

Granite Range

Located south of Jackpot at the headwaters of the Salmon Falls Creek, another Snake River tributary that once held salmon, lies the Granite Range. Although only a little more than 8,000 feet in elevation, they are composed of scenic granitic outcrops and boulders like those found at Joshua Tree National Monument in California.

Pilot Range

The only other high mountains in this part of Nevada are in the Pilot Range. Most of the range is in Utah, but Pilot Peak itself,

10,716 feet in elevation, is in Nevada. The mountain can be seen for miles and, in the early days of travel, expeditions crossing the northern Salt Lake desert would steer for this prominent and singular peak. John Frémont gave the summit its name in 1845, during his third expedition in the West. Elk, wandering in from nearby Utah, have established themselves here. In addition, 20 Rocky Mountain

bighorn sheep were reintroduced into the Miners Canyon area in 1987 and by 1991 a survey found that the herd had grown to 30 animals. The Pilot Range also is one of the northern reaches for white fir, a southern Rocky Mountain species.

CHAPTER SEVEN

EASTERN NEVADA

The entire Snake Range has been heavily glaciated and is sculpted with glacial cirques, arêtes and small lakes.

Eastern Nevada is, without exception, Nevada's premier mountain area. Ranges like the East Humboldt, Rubies, Schell Creek, Grant and White Pine are among the highest and most rugged mountains in the state. Yet the region is far from most urban centers and little known. The largest communities are Elko, Ely, Pioche and Wells.

Most, but not all of these mountains, are part of what is known as the limestone ranges, composed primarily of limestone and dolomite with occasional outcrops of metamorphosed rocks like quartzite and shale. All these rocks indicate formation under the sea and, indeed, for more than 300 million years the region—now uplifted as rocky limestone peaks—was part of a shallow sea along what was the western edge of the North American continent. Ranges largely of limestone origins include: Grant, Egan, Goshute, Pequop, White Pine, Butte, Bistol, Schell Creek and Snake. Even mountains that are overlain with volcanic rocks on the surface, like the Fortification and Wilson Creek ranges, have sedimentary formations as their bases.

Snake Range

The best known of the eastern Nevada mountains is the Snake Range, in part because Great Basin National Park encompasses part of the range. Areas outside the park are managed by either the Humboldt National Forest or the Bureau of Land Management. Sacramento Pass over which Highway 50 travels, divides the range into a north and south portion.

Wheeler Peak, 13,063 feet, the highest peak in the national park and southern half of the Snake Range, rises more than 8,000 feet above the Spring Valley—nearly a thousand feet more than the Grand Teton rises

above the Jackson Valley. Other high peaks include 12,298-foot Baker Peak, plus four other summits that rise above 11,000 feet. Although the majority of this range is limestone, the Wheeler Peak massif is composed of quartzite, a metamorphosed sandstone.

The entire Snake Range has been heavily glaciated and is sculpted with glacial cirques, arêtes and small lakes. Perhaps the most impressive is the Wheeler cirque, which has cliff walls towering 1,200 feet above the bottom of the glacially carved basin.

Although comparatively densely timbered (for the Great Basin), with forests of white fir, aspen, Engelmann spruce, Douglas fir and ponderosa pine, nearly 60 percent of the Wheeler Peak massif is treeless. Ancient bristlecone pines are scattered about the range, including what was once the oldest living tree on earth, a 4,900-year-old specimen which was chainsawed down in order to verify that it had been indeed the oldest thing alive. The Snake River also supports limber pine and lodgepole pine.

North of Sacramento Pass lies the northern half of the Snake Range. Its high point, 12,050-foot Mt. Moriah, Nevada's fifth-highest peak, is now part of the 82,000-acre Mt. Moriah Wilderness Area. As in the southern portion of the range, there are stands of bristlecone pine, particularly on the three-square-mile Table, a 10,500-foot-high plateau that lies north of the Mt. Moriah massif.

Schell Creek Range

Just east of Ely, and across the Spring Valley from the Snake Range, lies the Schell Creek Range, fourth-highest range in Nevada and one of the longest ranges in the state— 133 miles. Only one paved road crosses the entire range, Highway 50, at Connors Pass. The north-central portion of the range is part of the Humboldt National Forest, while the northernmost area and the rest of the southern portion are managed by the BLM. The bulk of the Schell Creeks are composed of limestone and other sedimentary rocks, but Tertiary age volcanic rocks crop out at the northern end.

Becky Peak, more than 10,000 feet in elevation, marks the northern end of the range, while a string of 11,000-foot-plus peaks including 11,883-foot North Schell Peak, the highest in the range, and 11,765-foot South Schell, the second-highest, make up a 20-mile section of the crest that lies continuously above timberline. A roadless area of more

Facing page: Aspen along Timber Creek, in the Schell Creek Range below North Schell Peak, Humboldt National Forest.

than 134,000 acres covering a large proportion of this highlands was proposed for wilderness as part of the 1989 Nevada Wilderness Bill, but unfortunately was never officially designated. This entire northern half has glacially carved basins and perennial streams, some with trout. The upper slopes are well forested with stands of pinyon pine, juniper, white fir, Engelmann spruce, Douglas fir, bristlecone pine, limber pine, and abundant groves of aspen that are especially beautiful in the autumn.

In the southern half lies 10,990-foot Mt.

Grafton, center of a 73,000-acre BLM wilderness study area and the highest peak on BLM lands in Nevada. A three-mile section of its summit lies above 10,000 feet and supports groves of bristlecone pine. Large groves of aspen, plus stands of ponderosa pine, unusual in much of Nevada, are found here.

Elk from Yellowstone National Park were transplanted into the Schell Creeks in 1932 and today an estimated 1,000 or more of their descendents live here and have colonized adjacent ranges like the Egan, White Pine and Snake.

Aspens are particularly abundant, adding much color in the fall.

Fortification, Wilson Creek, Egan ranges

South of Connors Pass and east of Highway 93 in the Lake Valley lies the 21-mile-long Fortification Range, whose highest peak is 8,532 feet. Unlike others in the region, this range is mostly composed of Tertiary volcanic flows cover most of the older sedimentary rocks. The range gets its name from volcanic rock eroded in columns and towers. The head of Cottonwood Creek is particularly scenic, with its spectacular cliffs.

The Wilson Creek Range, composed of volcanic white and pink Tertiary age tuffs, lies east of Pioche on the Utah border. Of several peaks above 9,000 feet, the highest is Mt. Wilson at 9,315 feet in elevation. The area has some "hoodoos" (naturally-carved columns in unusual shapes), exceptional archaeological sites, a small elk herd and successfully-reproducing ponderosa pine groves. Aspens are particularly abundant, adding much color in the fall. Two BLM wilderness

study areas encompassing 36,000 and 88,000 acres are located in this range.

To the west of the Schell Creeks across the Steptoe Valley lies the 110-mile-long Egan Range, named for Mormon settler and trader Howard Egan. Spectacular limestone cliffs are notable on the west side of the range south of Ely between Brown Knoll and Sheep Pass Canyon. The highest point is 10,936-foot South Ward Mountain. Nearly 150,000 acres in two units in the southern part of the range are being studied by the BLM as potential wilderness.

Like much of the country, pinyon-juniper covers the lower slopes of the Egan Range, while forests of ponderosa pine, white fir, aspen, Engelmann spruce limber pine and bristlecone pine are found at higher elevations. One unusual feature is a mixture of bristlecone and ponderosa pine together in the same stand. One of the densest populations of nesting prairie falcons in the region, plus recently reintroduced desert bighorn sheep, are other features of the range.

The Egan Range, like others in the region, is primarily sedimentary limestones and dolomites, but there are also intrusions of granitic bodies and their associated minerals, including the gold that was mined at Ward and the copper that helped to keep Ely alive for more than 50 years.

Cherry Creek Range, Goshute Mountains

North of Ely and across the Steptoe Valley from the Schell Creeks is the 40-mile-long Cherry Creek Range, composed primarily of limestone, dolomite and shales. The highest summit, Cherry Creek Peak, is 10,458 feet in elevation. Gold was discovered here in 1861 and by the 1880s the town of Cherry Creek was booming.

One of the attractions of the Cherry Creeks is Goshute Canyon, which harbors pure strains of Bonneville cutthroat trout, an endangered species. The area also supports a diverse and rich number of raptor species, including prairie falcons, Cooper's hawk, golden eagles and kestrels.

Not to be confused with the canyon of the same name are the Goshute Mountains, which lie 100 miles east of Elko near the Utah border. This 40-mile-long range rises nearly 5,300 feet above the Great Salt Lake Desert to 9,611-foot Goshute Peak, its highest peak. Named for the Goshute Indians, a branch of the Shoshone tribe, this fault-block limestone mass is best known as a major migration route for raptors. In autumn, hundreds of golden eagles, red-tailed hawks, goshawks, Cooper's hawks and kestrels can be seen in a single day, as they follow this ridge complex southward. Forests of white fir, lim-

Above: *Sunrise on the eastern flank of the East Humboldt Range below Chimney Rock Peak. East Humboldt Wilderness, Humboldt National Forest.*

Facing page: *Currant Mountain Wilderness in the White Pine Range, Humboldt National Forest.*

ber pine, bristlecone pine, pinyon and juniper cover the slopes. Two BLM wilderness study areas, 55,665 and 69,770 acres respectively, together encompass a major part of the Goshutes.

Ruby Mountains

Southwest of Elko lies one of Nevada's most majestic mountain ranges, the Rocky Mountains, locally called the Ruby Mountains. The eastern flank is abrupt and rises sharply from the Ruby Valley, while the western slope is gentler, but with deep, glaciated canyons. No other mountain range in the state is so sculpted and carved by glacial ice, featuring an abundance of glacial tarns, lakes and cirque basins. Unlike many other ranges in this region, the Rubies are primarily metamorphic rock—gneiss, marble and quartzite,

with outcrops of granitic rocks here and there, but few sedimentary limestones, except on the southern end.

Nearly 100 miles long, but seldom more than eight or ten miles wide, with their greatest width 16 miles, the Rubies are classic Basin and Range Province—long, linear mountains. And overall they are a high range, with Ruby Dome at 11,387 feet the apex. Other high peaks, all clustered around the center of the range, include 11,047-foot Verdi Peak and 11,316-foot Thomas Peak. The 90,000-acre Ruby Mountain Wilderness Area, with 40-mile-long Ruby Crest Trail running its length, takes in many of these higher peaks. A 23,000-acre roadless area south of Harrison Pass centered on 10,847-foot Pearl Peak was also proposed for wilderness, but still awaits official designation. It contains Nevada's northernmost grove of bristlecone pine.

Perhaps due to their height and isolation, the Rubies get more precipitation than most Basin and Range mountains and, with their wet, flower-studded meadows, seem more like a mountain range in the Rockies than a Great Basin range. Indeed, they have a larger share of alpine tundra than any other range in Nevada, with 189 plant species considered to be alpine varieties. Due to their isolation, the Rubies have only a few tree species—limber and whitebark pine, white fir, Engelmann spruce and extensive groves of aspen. A similar depauperate wildlife cohort characterizes this area as well, with elk, pine marten, black bear, and a host of other species absent. Rocky Mountain goats, never native to the range, have been introduced and today a small herd scampers among the high peaks.

The most tragic episode in the wildlife history of the Rubies was the loss of the range's bighorn sheep—the last ones were seen in 1921. Disease transmitted from domestic sheep was the most likely cause of their decline. Recently the

Crescent moon rises over Quinn Canyon Wilderness as seen near Cherry Creek Pass. Quinn Canyon Range, Humboldt National Forest.

Above: Looking up Lamoille Canyon, a glaciated U-shaped valley in the Ruby Mountains.

Facing page: Volcanic boulders in the Goshute Mountains, a major hawk migration corridor in autumn.

state of Nevada has reintroduced 45 Rocky Mountain bighorns into the range, most of the animals released in the Lee area on the west slope. Efforts to establish bighorns farther south near Pearl Peak have been hampered by the presence of domestic sheep, which still are permitted to graze public lands in the ranges.

East Humboldt, White Pine ranges

Just off Interstate 80 at Wells is the East Humboldt Range, a northern extension of the Rubies. Like the Rubies they are heavily glaciated and feature arêtes, cirques and small glacial lakes. The highest peaks are above 11,000 feet, with 11,306-foot Hole-in-the-Mountain Peak the tallest. Some 36,900 acres of the range is now part of the East Humboldt Range Wilderness Area.

Lying west of Ruth and Ely, the narrow, serrated, spine-like limestone crest of the White Pine Range has at least four peaks that exceed 11,000 feet, including 11,513-foot Currant Mountain, now part of the 36,000-acre Currant Mountain Wilderness Area. The rocky backbone of the range is home to ancient bristlecone pine and bighorn sheep. Despite its name, there is no white pine in the White Pine Range, although forests of white fir, Engelmann spruce and limber pine cloak the higher parts of the range, while pinyon-juniper dominates lower slopes. The woodlands of this 50-mile-long range provided the raw material that went into building the nearby mining towns of Hamilton and Shermantown.

Grant and Quinn Canyon ranges

Lying south of the White Pine Range are the twin uplifts of the Grant and Quinn Canyon ranges. Cherry Creek Canyon separates them but in reality they should be considered as one range. The highest parts of both are part of the Humboldt National Forest, while lower elevations are managed by the BLM. Beginning at the hamlet of Currant and extending south for 80 miles, this spectacular and rugged range has a maximum total relief

of 6,600 feet above the adjacent Railroad Valley, with 11,298-foot Troy Peak as the highest summit, plus several other 11,000-foot-plus peaks.

Like others in this region, the Grant Range is largely an uplifted limestone block. Mineralized centers of volcanic rock outcrops, however, occur here and there. The Troy Mining District on Troy Creek is one such area that produced gold, silver and tungsten. The mountains south of Cherry Creek in the Quinn Canyon Range are largely volcanic, with some outcrops forming rocky reddish

turrets and steep-walled canyons. Due to the presence of non-absorbent volcanic rock, this southern area tends to have more surface water than in the largely limestone areas to the north.

Special features of the range include one of the largest bighorn sheep herds in the region. They are mostly the Rocky Mountain variety, but the northernmost herd of desert bighorn lives at the southern end of the Quinn Canyon Range. In addition, some of the best developed white fir and aspen forests in eastern Nevada are found in some of the Grant Range's eastern canyons, while tall ponderosa pines grow in Big Creek Canyon. On the higher ridges flourish groves of bristlecone pine. Scofield Canyon, in the Grant

Range, is particularly beautiful, not only because of its dense forest but also because it is one of the few places in Nevada where domestic livestock grazing does not occur. The vegetation here is lush and thick, and gives some indication of what much of Nevada could look like if the scourge of domestic livestock were removed from the public lands.

The 59,560-acre Blue Eagle BLM wilderness study area lies in the northern end of the range, immediately adjacent to the 57,000-acre Riordan's Well BLM WSA. Both are dominated by high limestone cliffs, abundant forests and a maze of peaks. The middle section surrounding Troy Peak is now protected as the 50,000-acre Grant Range Wilderness Area, while the 27,000-acre Quinn Canyon Wilderness Area takes in a portion of the southern end of this mountain block.

Right: *Aspen along Schell Creek Range in Timber Canyon, Humboldt National Forest.*
Below: *Aerial view of Big Wash Canyon in the Snake Range.*
JEFF GNASS PHOTO

Sunrise touches Marys River Peak and Emerald Lake in the Jarbidge Wilderness. JEFF GNASS PHOTO

GREAT BASIN NATIONAL PARK

Above: White fir needles.

Facing page, top: Lexington Arch in Arch Canyon, Great Basin National Park. JEFF GNASS PHOTO

Bottom: Hiker gives scale to wind-sheared limber pine and Englemann spruce on Bald Mountain, Great Basin National Park.

Great Basin National Park (GBNP) is our newest national park, established in 1986 and located in eastern Nevada's Snake Range, a rugged jumble of mountains that rises nearly 8,000 feet above the surrounding valley floors. Centerpiece of the park is 13,063-foot Wheeler Peak, Nevada's second-highest peak, and the highest one in a 500-mile west-east path between the California border and the Uinta Range in Utah. Thirteen other peaks in the park also rise above 11,000 feet, making this one of the highest ranges of the entire Great Basin. Although the new park includes a good representation of the Snake Range, it does not—despite its name—include any of the adjacent basin environment.

Also included in the park are Lehman Caves, which previously were a separate national park unit 640 acres in size. Currently, this area still gets the most visitors within the new park, with more than 50,000 people a year. Among the features that can be seen on guided tours through the cave are cave coral, shields, helicites, stalagmites and stalactites.

Within the park are representations of a wide diversity of plant communities. Lower elevations consist of pinyon-juniper woodland, various saltbush and sagebrush species, plus mountain mahogany. At higher elevations are more continuous forests that resemble in many ways the forests found in the Rocky Mountains to the east. These include Engelmann spruce, white fir, some relict ponderosa pine and Douglas fir, plus aspen and limber pine. Among the park's trademarks are the three groves of bristlecone pine found near timberline. At the highest elevations, making up 8 percent of the park, is alpine tundra. A number of rare and endemic plant species occur in the park, including at least seven candidates for listing as endangered species.

Wildlife in the park include a small relict herd of bighorn sheep, and Bonneville cutthroat trout, an endangered species, found in Pine and Ridge creeks. Also found in GBNP are mule deer, mountain lion, bobcat, ring-tailed cat, badger, weasel, jackrabbit, beaver, red fox, coyote, and a wide variety of smaller mammals. The koret checkerspot butterfly, endemic to the Snake Range, may be seen here.

Elk once roamed the Snake Range, but were extirpated in the 1800s. However, elk reintroduced into the Schell Creek Range have expanded their range, and transients occasionally wander into the South Snake Range. In the not too distant future, elk may reestablish breeding populations here.

The Snake Range is made up of quartzite, a metamorphic sandstone, along with limestones—Lehman Cave, for example, is a cavern within the limestone layer. The limestones were deposited in a warm, shallow sea between 600 and 245 million years ago.

Between 245 and 67 million years ago, the area that is now the Snake Range was uplifted, and erosion began to remove some of the rock layers. About 17 million years ago, the earth in the entire Great Basin began to stretch and pull apart, cracking the crust into north-south blocks with valleys and ranges, one of which is the Snake Range.

Two million years ago the Pleistocene Ice Age began. Lakes occupied valleys on both sides of the Snake Range and glaciers sculpted the higher peaks, including the massive cirque evident today on the north face of Wheeler Peak. This same cirque holds the only existing glacier left in the Great Basin. There are six subalpine lakes in the park, all on the east side of the range.

Creating a Park

Fur trapper Jedediah Smith was probably the first European to see what is now Great Basin National Park. Traversing the Great Basin from California back to Wyoming in June of 1827, Smith crossed Spring Valley and the Snake Range, no doubt by way of Sacramento Pass.

The next explorers to enter what is now the park were a party of Mormons who in 1855 climbed Wheeler Peak. Various military expeditions recorded references to the peak and, in 1878, John Muir, founder of the Sierra Club, himself climbed Wheeler Peak.

By the time Muir ambled up Wheeler, miners and ranchers were already established in the area, doing business and building towns. By the turn of the century, overgrazing by large unregulated herds of sheep and cattle had turned many mountain pastures into dust, and choked streams with sediment. To bring some regulation to the grazing industry, Theodore Roosevelt established the Nevada National Forest in 1909, its land including what is now Great Basin National Park.

The next change in land management policy occurred in the 1920s, when Lehman Caves were

recommended as a new national monument. The original monument boundaries were to encompass fewer than 6,000 acres, but local ranchers objected, suggesting this removed too much land from their grazing base. (They had only the rest of the entire states of Utah and Nevada available for grazing.) Acting upon local pressure, the monument size was scaled down to a paltry 640 acres and, in 1922, Lehman Caves National Monument was carved out of lands administered by the Nevada National Forest.

In 1924, shortly after the caves were given national monument status, Senator Key Pittman of Nevada put forth a proposal to expand the monument into a national park taking in Wheeler Peak and other parts of the Snake Range. But opposition from local ranchers killed the idea.

In 1933, Senator James G. Scrugham asked the National Park Service to study several sites in Nevada for potential national park status. Great Basin National Park was again recommended,

Above: Aerial view of sunrise on Wheeler Peak and Jeff Davis Peak (left) in the Snake Range.

Right: In the Grand Palace in Lehman Caves.
JEFF GNASS PHOTOS

but the proposal died with Senator Scrugham, who passed away in mid-term.

Then in the 1950s, momentum for a national park again surfaced, drawing local support from the White Pine County Chamber of Commerce, as well as national groups like the National Parks and Conservation Association, Sierra Club and The Wilderness Society. In 1955, advocates came up with another park proposal: expand Lehman Caves National Monument, incorporate more of the Snake Range, and name the area Great Basin National Park.

The Forest Service, now administering the area as part of the Humboldt National Forest, countered this plan by establishing a 28,000-acre Wheeler Peak Scenic Area. Its officials also proposed building a two-lane road up to Stella Lake, building a ski resort and leasing public lands for summer homes.

Then, in 1965, a new idea for a national recreation area gained some popular support. A tramway would be built from Lehman Caves toward Wheeler Peak, a ski resort established, and grazing, hunting and mining would continue as usual. Many conservationists felt this idea was merely another dodge designed to sidetrack national park proposals.

In the early 1970s, a new study was ordered by Congress to determine where, or whether, a Great Basin National Park should be created. Once again the Snake Range was studied, along with the White Mountains and Fish Lake Valley, the Monitor Range and Big Smoky Valley, and the Railroad Valley. The Snake Range was ranked highest, fueling new efforts for a national park centered on Lehman Caves and Wheeler Peak.

By the mid-1980s it appeared almost certain that some kind of park bill would be passed, but proposals introduced into Congress recommended acreages ranging from 174,000 to 44,000 acres.

Besides the proposed size of the park, there were other problems to consider. Much debate hinged on livestock grazing. There were five individual permittees whose livestock grazed in the proposed park, including one California corporation. The debate centered on the goals and ideals behind national parks. Livestock grazing usually is not allowed on national park lands, and where it does still occur, it is typically scheduled for eventual termination. The rationale is that parks are supposed to preserve native species and ecosystems. Since domestic livestock are not only exotic, alien species, but often are destructive to natural ecosystem, continuing such an obviously incompatible use is seldom permitted.

Furthermore, one of the recognized values of national parks, and one of the justifications for establishment of Great Basin National Park, is to provide baseline landscapes where no human manipulation occurs. Since almost no place of any size in the entire Great Basin is not grazed by domestic livestock, termination of grazing permits in the Park would be of great scientific value, providing a "control" where people could see how this type of ecosystem might function in the absence of domestic animals.

Eventually, the compromise enacted in October 1986 called for creation of a 77,086-acre park, with livestock grazing to continue as permitted on July 1, 1985, with no scheduled termination.

Park Enhancement

As a national preserve of the Great Basin ecosystem, Great Basin National Park has two serious flaws that greatly compromise its value and integrity as a national park unit and nature preserve.

The first problem is the previously mentioned presence of livestock. Cattle and domestic sheep not only eat forage and use space and water that would otherwise support native species, but also they can pollute water supplies, introduce non-native plant species, introduce disease to native wild species (disease from domestic sheep that still graze in the park may be the cause of a decline in wild bighorns residing here), and do considerable damage to soils, riparian areas and other sensitive locations.

The second flaw with the present park is one of size. Numerous studies in the past decade have demonstrated that natural reserves must have a minimum size to effectively preserve biological diversity and allow for dynamic ecological processes. A 1985 study by William Newmark concluded that most western national parks, even large ones like Yellowstone, are too small to maintain minimum viable populations of some species for even 100 years. Unless expanded greatly, Great Basin National Park, as a biological preserve, will ultimately fail.

At the least, adding one of the adjacent valleys and one more range would greatly enhance the park's ecological value. For example, the boundaries could be expanded to take in the Spring Valley and Schell Creek Range as well as the Snake Range. Only then will we have protected a true representation of the Great Basin. When the National Park Service conducted its study of the proposed Great Basin National Park in the 1970s, it had included just about this area in its 811,000-acre study boundaries. Such an expansion would make Great Basin National Park not only biologically viable, but also worthy as a representation of what the Great Basin ecosystems really have to offer.

Numerous studies in the past decade have demonstrated that natural reserves must have a minimum size to effectively preserve biological diversity and allow for dynamic ecological processes.

Views of Great Basin National Park:
Right: *A Snake Creek Canyon aspen sports souvenirs of thoughtless long-ago visitors.* JEFF GNASS PHOTO
Below: *Curl-leaf mountain mahogany.*
Bottom: *Winter sunrise on the Snake Range as seen from Baker.*

Facing page: *Glacial cirque and the only known glacier in the Great Basin lie against Wheeler Peak's north flank.*

CHAPTER EIGHT

CENTRAL NEVADA

Here in Central Nevada is the classic heart of the Great Basin, rising higher than the basin's outer edges.

The Great Basin is bowed, with its outer edges lower than its middle. In this center lies some of Nevada's highest mountain terrain. This region, south of the Humboldt River and generally north of Highway 6, sandwiched between the calcareous mountains on the east and the Lahontan Trough on the west, is the classic heart of the Great Basin. The largest communities within the region are Austin, Eureka, Gabbs and Fallon while Tonopah, Hawthorne, Elko, Carlin, Battle Mountain, Winnemucca and Lovelock define the outer bounds.

These highlands, such as the Shoshone, Toiyabe, Monitor and Toquima ranges, are among the longest in the state and are positioned between the Sierra Nevada and the Rockies. No ponderosa pine or Engelmann spruce here. The Toiyabe, Shoshone, Paradise, Monitor and Toquima ranges are within the Toiyabe National Forest, while the lower elevations and nearly all the region's other mountains are controlled by the Bureau of Land Management. Unlike in ranges farther east, sedimentary outcrops are relatively rare among these ranges, while mountains of volcanic origin are far more common—with some, like the Toiyabe and Stillwater, being a mixture of all three major rock types—igneous, metamorphic and sedimentary.

Pancake, Hot Creek ranges

Beginning in the Great Basin's southeast corner, the first range encountered is 74-mile-long Pancake Range—named for its repeated layering of volcanic rock that is said to resemble a stack of pancakes. Its highest summit is 9,240-foot Portuguese Mountain. Near the southern tip of the range is Lunar Crater, a region of fresh volcanic cinder cones, lava flows and craters that erupted only a few thousand years ago. The crater, formed by the explosive release of gases, is listed on the National Natural Landmark Register.

Directly west across the Hot Creek Valley and east of the Stone Cabin Valley is the 50-mile-long Hot Creek Range. Extending north from Long Canyon the 25-mile-long Antelope Range can be considered a northern extension of the Hot Creeks.

The range is forested with pinyon, juniper, aspen and limber pine, with small groves of bristlecone pine on 10,246-foot Morey Peak, the highest summit and one of two locations where bristlecone pine is known to grow on volcanic soils. Morey Peak is thought to be a collapsed volcanic caldera composed of welded tuff and ash.

South Six Mile Creek, a perennial stream, provides a diversity of riparian habitat and sustains a small population of trout. Bighorn sheep were recently reintroduced into the range. A special feature of the remote Antelope Range are pristine meadows never grazed by domestic livestock, an almost unknown feature in Nevada. Some of the higher meadows around Morey Peak also receive little livestock use. Within the combined Hot Creek and Antelope ranges are four large BLM wilderness study areas.

Monitor Range

Sixty miles northeast of Tonopah lies the hundred-mile-long Monitor Range, one of the major ranges of Nevada. Looking more like a mesa in Colorado, at the heart of the range lies Table Mountain, a 10-mile-long, aspen-covered plateau that rises gently from the west to an average height of 10,000 feet. (Its highest point is 10,888 feet.) Besides aspen, there are pockets of limber pine and mountain mahogany.

The 98,000-acre Table Mountain Wilderness Area is the third-largest designated wilderness in Nevada. With five perennial streams, the range has abundant water. One stream, Mosquito Creek, has populations of the endangered Lahonton cutthroat trout. Elk, not native to this part of Nevada, were introduced into the Monitor Range in 1979 and now number more than 300.

Roberts Mountains, Toquima Range

North of the Monitor Range lies the small, unassuming uplift of the Roberts Mountains. Compact and nearly round, instead of the lin-

Facing page: Aspen grow on glacial moraines in the cirque at the headwaters of the North Twin River, Arc Dome Wilderness, Toiyabe Range.

ear pattern typical of the Great Basin, it is known for one of the most important structural features in the entire intermountain West, the Roberts Mountains Thrust Fault. Nearly 600 million years ago, this was the western edge of the continent—land's end— where a warm, shallow sea lapped against the shore (see page 12). Today limestone dominates the range's high peak, such as 10,133-foot Roberts Creek Mountain. The

central Nevada's most impressive range—the 126-mile-long Toiyabe Range. For 50 miles of its length, the center spine of the range never drops below 10,000 feet, and the Toiyabe Crest Trail, a 72-mile-long designated National Scenic Trail and the longest maintained trail in Nevada, gives access to this remarkable area. This range rises

central portion of this range is part of a BLM wilderness study area.

Across the Monitor Valley is the Toquima Range, rising to 11,941 feet at the apex of its three-mile-long summit, Mt. Jefferson, the loftiest point in central Nevada, and sixth-highest peak in Nevada. Glaciated, it holds a number of cirque basins and even a small alpine lake at 11,000 feet. Lush riparian zones with water birch and aspen crowd waterways like Pine Creek, home to trout. At one time, Indians hunted bighorn sheep on the high slopes and even today a small herd of desert bighorn lives here. At the head of Pine Creek, at nearly 10,000 feet, are the remains of a sawmill that once cut limber pine for hauling to the nearby county seat of Belmont, now largely deserted. The 38,000-acre Alta Toquima Wilderness Area surrounds the Mt. Jefferson area and nearby slopes.

Toiyabe Range

North of Tonopah and across the Big Smoky Valley from the Toquima Range is

abruptly and dramatically from surrounding Big Smoky and Reese River valleys with its eastern escarpment looking particularly wall-like. The tallest peak, Arc Dome, towers 6,300 feet above the nearby lowlands, reaching 11,788 feet in elevation; it is the tenth-loftiest peak in Nevada. Other high peaks include 11,474-foot Bunker Hill, 11,361-foot Toiyabe Dome southeast summit, 10,793-foot Toiyabe Peak.

The geology of the Toiyabe Range is complex. Granite outcrops show here and there, such as between Ophir and Kingston Canyons, where the "Wild Granites" present a 4,000-foot wall of spires and columns. At the southern end of the range, though, the rock is made up of red

Above: *Sunset on saltbrush, Clan Alpine Range.*

Facing page: *Earthquake scarp indicates fault along the base of the Stillwater Range by Job Peak, as seen from the Dixie Valley.*

volcanic outcrops, remnants of an ancient volcanic crater. Elsewhere, sedimentary rocks are exposed, as in Kingston Canyon. Glaciation has sculpted some of the higher peaks in classic cirque basins.

Despite their tremendous elevational range, the Toiyabes—like most central Nevada mountains—are sometimes called the bald mountains. Besides the ubiquitous pinyon-juniper of lower elevations, they support mountain mahogany, aspen and limber pine. Many of the higher alpine areas are covered by a mixture of low sagebrush and an alpine flora of fewer than 50 species.

But height does have one advantage: the Toiyabe Range has an abundance of water—at least by central Great Basin standards. Small streams like the North and South Twin rivers, Peavine Creek, Stewart Creek, Reese River, Big Creek and Kingston Creek are all examples of lush riparian areas with an abundance of shrubs and trees like chokecherry, elderberry, red osier dogwood, cottonwood, aspen and water birch. All of these waters have trout, with both Stewart Creek and Reese River home to the endangered Lahontan cutthroat trout. Despite the biological and aesthetic values of these waterways, domestic livestock still is permitted to foul these otherwise clear streams.

One wonderful exception is Kingston Creek, where livestock grazing has been eliminated from the creek bottoms. The stream basin is densely cloaked in lush grasses, and the creek runs in a deep, narrow channel instead of the wide and shallow, cow-blasted, muddy banks one typically sees in Nevada. Here is a glaring reminder of what Nevada's streamside riparian areas *could* look like.

Competition and disease as a consequence of domestic sheep grazing (which still occurs) have eliminated the native bighorn from much of the range, but in the most rugged sections of the southern part of these mountains, a small herd of fewer than a hundred desert bighorn hangs on.

On the slopes of the Toiyabe Range sits Austin. In 1862, a Pony Express rider accidentally found a rich silver vein, setting off a stampede for the Toiyabes. By 1864, nearly 10,000 people were scouring the hills for more wealth or working the mines (or the miners for their money). Today Austin is quite a bit quieter, but it retains a flavor of its rich past.

From Austin southward, most of the higher elevations are part of the Toiyabe National Forest, while north of Austin, the entire range is under BLM management. The southernmost portion of the Toiyabe Range is now protected as part of the 115,000-acre Arc Dome Wilderness Area. A minimum of 225,000 additional acres in the southern and central portions of the range are equally as dramatic and wild. They could be designated as wilderness, including the entire length of the Toiyabe Crest Trail and the Bunker Hill area north of Kingston Creek.

Shoshone Mountains and Range

Immediately west of the Reese River Valley is one of Nevada's longest, if not most impressive, ranges, the Shoshone Mountains. The Reese River cuts through the range north of Austin, where the name changes to the Shoshone Range; this long chain of peaks, however, should be considered as one. Together the Shoshone Mountains and Range run 170 miles north from the Ione Valley to the Hum-

boldt River. Along its length, the highest point is 10,313-foot North Shoshone Peak.

Much of the range is built up of marine sedimentary rocks like limestone, as well as volcanic rocks of varying age, including some from massive lava and ash flows of the Tertiary period approximately 34 to 17 million years ago. Outcrops of quartz harbored the gold and silver that led to the establishment of Berlin (now a state-protected ghost town) in the southern part of the range.

Desatoya Mountains

West of the Shoshone Mountains and south of New Pass Summit lie the volcanic peaks of the Desatoya Mountains, peaks composed of welded tuffs of rhyolite. Sedimentary marine deposits of sandstone, shale and mudstone also occur. The highest point in this 36-mile-long range is 9,973-foot Desatoya Peak.

The Desatoyas are watered by 11 perennial streams, making this one of the better-wa-

In 1862, a Pony Express rider accidentally found a rich silver vein, setting off a stampede for the Toiyabes.

tered mountains in central Nevada. Several of these streams are home to Humboldt cutthroat trout. Lush riparian areas of willows, aspens, ferns and wildflowers mark each of these waterways. Except for juniper-pinyon woodlands, which cover approximately 50 percent of the range, and isolated stands of mountain mahogany, there are no other tree species in this range. The higher-elevation ridges are covered with grass and low sagebrush.

One small animal found here is the pika, a small rabbit-like mammal whose distribution

Desert bighorn sheep have been reintroduced into the Desatoya Mountains and the herd now numbers an estimated 75 individuals.

on higher mountains throughout the Great Basin is disjunct and spotty. Desert bighorn sheep have been reintroduced and the herd now numbers an estimated 75 individuals. Ruins of the Cold Spring Pony Express station lie on the northern edge of the range. A 51,000-acre roadless area has been studied by the BLM as potential wilderness.

Clan Alpine Mountains

Immediately west and slightly north of the Desatoya Mountains are the 50-mile-long Clan Alpine Mountains, which are bounded by the Edwards Creek and Dixie valleys. Rising an impressive 6,300 feet above the Dixie Valley is 9,966-foot Mt. Augusta, the highest summit. From the top of the range, the Sierra Nevada can frequently be seen a hundred miles away.

The main mountain block is composed of sedimentary rocks, but there are also granitic outcrops and, adding to the scenic quality are colorful Tertiary age volcanic flows, tuffs and welded tuffs. Hot springs occur in the Dixie Valley immediately adjacent to the range.

Trout live in Horse Creek, one of five perennial streams running down from the

heights. A small herd of desert bighorn sheep was reintroduced into the range in 1986. The BLM is studying part of the area for possible wilderness designation.

Stillwater Range

During the last Ice Age, the 75-mile-long Stillwater Range was a peninsula surrounded by the waters of glacial Lake Lahontan. The valleys surrounding it, including the Dixie Valley on the east and the Carson Sink and Stillwater National Wildlife Refuge near Fallon on the west, are now the dried-up lake bottoms. The lowlands surrounding the range are part of the Lahontan Trough, which permits desert species from southern Nevada to invade farther north than in any other part of Nevada. In these lowlands, shadscale and saltbush are common, as well as southern animal species like the kit fox, Ord's kangaroo rat, long-tailed pocket mouse and Botta's pocket gopher. A growing herd of more than 120 desert bighorn sheep are known to inhabit the range, and at least part of their territory is included in one of two BLM wilderness study areas of nearly 200,000 acres centered on the range.

The range is a composite of different rock types including slate and schist and is overlaid with volcanic rocks. The steep eastern escarpment of the range is still rising. Earthquakes in 1903, 1954 and 1964 rocked the area, and an impressive 6- to 10-foot-tall fault scarp can easily be seen from the Dixie Valley especially below 8,790-foot Job Peak, the highest in the range. The deep faulting allows water to come in contact with heat, and the geothermal potential of the area is high, as evidenced by the abundance of hot springs in the Dixie Valley.

Four-hundred-foot Sand Mountain lies cradled against the southwest flank of the range. The sand dune, a favorite place for dune buggy riders, is composed of sands that once lay at the bottom of Lake Lahontan.

Ruins of the Sand Mountain Pony Express station can be seen here as well. Between April 3, 1860 and October 28, 1861, the pony express carried the mail by horseback from St. Joseph, to Sacramento, California for $5 per letter. The 1,800-mile distance was covered in 10 days if all went well. All did not always go well though and Indians, weather and bandits were only some of the perils faced by the riders. Pony Express riders were usually young, very light weight, and expert riders. Orphans were preferred. This shortlived enterprise went out of business with the completion of the first transcontinental telegraph line.

Humboldt Range

Just south of Rye Patch Reservoir and easily seen from Interstate 80 lies the 40-mile-long Humboldt Range, rising 5,700 feet above the Humboldt River to its greatest elevation of 9,834 feet at Star Peak. The range has been a source of mineral wealth for more than a hundred years. Perhaps the best known gold camp was Unionville, established after gold was discovered in the central Humboldt Range in 1861. At its height, Unionville boasted 2,000 to 3,000 residents and was the seat of Humboldt County.

Above: *Abandoned ranch in Reese River Valley. The view is toward the 125-mile-long Toiyabe Range.*

Facing page: *Humboldt Sink, where the Humboldt River drains, and its giant playa.*

CHAPTER NINE

SOUTHERN NEVADA

Southern Nevada is surprisingly diverse, supporting 43 percent of all species recorded for the state.

The southern region of Nevada is basically outlined by the Mojave Desert. This includes everything south of a line from the White Mountains on the California border, east through Tonopah, south of the Quinn Canyon Range to Caliente near the Utah border. Las Vegas is the major population center. Lower in elevation than central or northern Nevada, this region is hotter and drier, and to many seems bleak. But southern Nevada is surprisingly diverse, supporting 43 percent of all species recorded for the state. This is, in part, due to its mountains, which rise up above the desert heat and so serve as island outposts for northern-forest species.

The lowest elevations and valleys have vegetation characteristic of the Mojave, dominated by creosote bush, saltbush, blackbrush, shadscale, and various cactus and yuccas including the Joshua tree. At slightly higher elevations, one encounters sagebrush and rabbitbrush more typical of central and northern Nevada. Many southern mountain ranges do not rise high enough to support other higher-elevation vegetation types. But the highest ranges receive enough moisture, mostly as snow, to host forests of juniper, pinyon, aspen, and even pine and fir. Common desert animals—rare or unusual farther north—include desert tortoise, gray fox, kit fox, roadrunner, Gambel's quail, cactus wren, ringtail cat, collared lizard and gila woodpecker.

Spring Mountains

Without question, the title of most dramatic range in the region goes to the Spring Mountains, named for the numerous springs that well up throughout the area—although one could suggest the name also could apply to how this mountain range seems to spring from the surrounding lowlands. Rising more than two miles above the valley floor, the Springs possess the greatest relief of any mountain area in Nevada. Charleston Peak, the highest summit and eighth-highest peak in Nevada, is 11,912 feet in elevation. On a clear day, from the summit it's possible to see more than 200 miles, even to the Sierra Nevada in California. Other high peaks include 11,530-foot Mummy Mountain, 11,072-foot Griffith Peak, and 10,772-foot McFarland Peak.

This 80-mile-long range, which begins near the California border, trends north and then northwest. It is bounded on the east by the Las Vegas Valley and on the west by the Pahrump Valley. The Spring Mountains are well known for the Keystone Thrust, a major fault that drove gray older Paleozoic limestones and dolomites up and over red younger Mesozoic beds of Aztec sandstone. This layering sequence is readily evident in Red Rock Canyon National Conservation Area. To anyone familiar with the sandstone canyons of southern Utah, the red Aztec sandstone of Red Rock Canyon looks very familiar. It should—it is the same rock. The Aztec sandstone is fossilized sand dunes.

As you ascend the range, you pass from typical Mojave desert vegetation like Joshua tree and barrel cactus up through the pinyon-juniper belt, and then encounter Pleistocene relict forest species like ponderosa pine, white fir, aspen and the most extensive stand of bristlecone pine—18,000 acres in size—in Nevada. Disjunct occurrences of species found in other regions include Gambel's oak which is common in the Rockies and southwest, as well as sword fern typically associated with wet Pacific Northwest rainforests.

Isolated as they are, the Spring Mountains have at least 30 endemic species, including Charleston angelica, Keck's penstemon and Clokey's thistle (two subalpine species found on the mountain's highest ridges), plus Nevada's only endemic mammal—the Palmer chipmunk—and the Spring Mountain blue butterfly. Elk, never native to the area, were introduced in the 1930s. One observer remembered that, in the early 1900s, both deer and bighorn sheep were abundant in the Spring Mountains and recalls seeing a migration across the Las Vegas Valley of more than a thousand bighorns between the Spring Mountains and Sheep Mountains to the east.

Left: A January morning in the Spring Mountains. JEFF GNASS PHOTO

Above: Ruins at the ghost town of Rhyolite near the Bullfrog Hills.

Facing page: Sunset glow on a Joshua tree below the Sheep Range, sedimentary limestone mountains in the Desert Wildlife Refuge.

Today approximately 160 desert bighorn are thought to roam the central and southern portion of the range.

Toiyabe National Forest

Today, the Spring Mountains are a part of the Toiyabe National Forest, following various administrative designations over the years. Some 43,000 acres of the highest ridges and peaks are protected within the Mt. Charleston Wilderness Area managed by the Toiyabe National Forest. Three other major Bureau of Land Management roadless areas straddle the range, including the 69,000-acre Mt. Stirling wilderness study area on the northern end of the range, the 56,000-acre La Madre Mountains WSA, and the 24,000-acre Pine Creek WSA, which dominate the central portion of the range within the BLM's Red Rock Canyon National Conservation Area. The combined Forest Service and BLM roadless areas make up a unit of nearly 230,000 acres.

Desert Wildlife Refuge and Sheep Mountain Range

Just north of Las Vegas and directly across the Las Vegas Valley from the Spring Mountains lies the Desert Wildlife Refuge, at 1.5 million acres the largest wildlife refuge in the lower 48 states. The western half of the refuge is used as a gunnery and bombing range by Nellis Air Force Base and is not open to the public.

Originally, the Sheep Range was part of the national forest system, but the Forest Service lost control of the area when the refuge was established in 1936, primarily to protect desert bighorn sheep. Indeed, more desert bighorn are found here than anywhere else in the world—a minimum of 1,500 sheep are thought to wander the refuge's six mountain ranges, the highest, longest and largest range being appropriately known as the Sheep Range.

The Sheep Range, along with others in the refuge like the Las Vegas, Pintwater and Desert ranges, are all fault-block, uplifted masses of limestone.

The Sheep Range sprawls northward some 50 miles and is as many as 12 miles wide. Rising nearly 6,000 feet in precipitous, tiered cliffs and rugged, turreted canyons above the surrounding lowlands, the highest peak is 9,912-foot Hayford Peak, while Sheep Peak, the second-highest in the range, is 9,750 feet. The other ranges are considerably lower. The highest elevation in the Las Vegas Range is 7,133-foot Quartzite Mountain—and both the Desert Range and Pintwater Range are of nearly equal elevation.

Corn Creek Springs, at the Desert Wildlife Refuge headquarters, is a genuine oasis in the desert with reed ponds, cottonwood trees, and an abundance of birds—more than 200 species have been recorded here. The ponds are also home to the Pahrump poolfish, a minnow-sized species transplanted here after its native home in the Pahrump Valley was destroyed by ground-water pumping.

Beyond the influence of the springs, typical Mojave Desert vegetation cloaks the valleys and lower slopes, primarily creosote bush, white bursage, Mojave yucca, and various cactus. At between 4,000 and 6,000 feet, blackbrush and Joshua tree woodlands take over, while pinyon-juniper woodlands and sagebrush are abundant between 6,000 and 7,000 feet. Only the highest peaks in the Sheep Range, above 7,000 feet, hold coniferous forests of white fir and ponderosa pine. Bristlecone pine crowns the summits just below 10,000 feet.

Kawich Range

North of the Desert Wildlife Refuge and Nellis Air Force Range and east of Tonopah lies the rugged 56-mile-long Kawich Range. It features deep canyons and colorful rocky outcrops, and its highest summit, Kawich Peak, reaches 9,404 feet skyward. Forests of pinyon-juniper are found on the higher elevations. Some 54,000 acres are included in a BLM wilderness study area.

Reveille, Silver Peak ranges

Immediately east of the Kawich Range is the Reveille Range, composed primarily of basalts and other extrusive volcanic rocks. This 30-mile-long desert range is extremely rugged with a crest of sharp peaks. Some of

Corn Creek Springs, at the Desert Wildlife Refuge headquarters, is a genuine oasis in the desert with reed ponds, cottonwood trees, and an abundance of birds.

the canyons are a thousand feet deep with cliffs hundreds of feet high. The highest point is 8,910-foot Reveille Peak. One prominent feature is the sawtoothed summit of Fang Ridge, which has a series of rhyolite spires 200-300 feet high. More than 100,000 acres are roadless and included in a BLM wilderness study area.

Southwest of Tonopah, near the California border, is the Silver Peak Range, the largest mountain uplift in Esmeralda County. Its main ridgeline runs nearly 40 miles southward until it merges with the Palmetto Mountains. The highest summit is 9,450-foot Piper Peak, a three-mile-long, treeless summit plateau, but the range's namesake, Silver Peak

is only slightly lower at 9,376 feet. Just below these peaks grows a band of pinyon-juniper woodland; otherwise the rest of the range is cloaked in desert shrubs like shadscale, blackbrush and saltbush.

Two spectacular canyons, Piper and Icehouse, penetrate the Silver Peak Range

The Silver Peak Range is home to the endangered spotted bat, a species that must have both roosting caves and water sources close by.

and reveal colorful pink, white, and green volcanic tuffs. The range's volcanic past is evident in a four-mile by eight-mile collapsed magma chamber, the Silver Peak caldera, now partially buried under more recent lava flows. In addition, pebbles of obsidian and even petrified wood can be found in some locations.

The range has seven perennial water sources, one reason it has one of the largest desert bighorn sheep herds in southern Nevada. It is also home to the endangered spotted bat, a species that must have both roosting caves and water sources close by. These requirements are met in the Silver Peak Range. Some 33,000 acres of the Silver Peak Range are currently under study by the BLM for potential wilderness designation.

Grapevine Mountains

South of the Silver Peak Range and 20 miles northwest of Beatty, on the California border in Death Valley National Monument, are the Grapevine Mountains. Sometimes, along with the Funeral and Black mountains, they are collectively known as the Amargosa Range. The Grapevine segment is 34 miles long, half of which is in Nevada. After the

Spring Mountains, this range has the greatest vertical relief in the state, rising more than 9,000 feet above Death Valley, with 8,740-foot Grapevine Peak the highest summit. This volcanic range is composed of dacites, rhyolites, andesites, and tuffs, often of colorful hues. Sweeping bajadas slope away from the range to the valley floors. Vegetation is composed of typical Mojave Desert shrubs, such as creosote bush and Joshua tree, although pinyon-juniper woodland occurs on the highest elevations.

Desert mountain ranges

South of Las Vegas and Interstate 15 in Clark County, where Nevada is squeezed like a wedge between Arizona and California, lie three low desert ranges—the McCullough Range, El Dorado Mountains, and Newberry Mountains. The McCullough is the most westerly and forms a long, narrow ridge, seldom more than three to five miles wide. Flat or rounded Tertiary-age volcanic peaks form the narrow northern section, while the southern portion, separated by a broad pass, is wider and consists of metamorphosed Precambrian rock—primarily gneiss, granite and schist. The highest point is 7,026-foot McCullough Mountain. Two BLM wilderness study areas, one in the north and a second in the south, are being considered for wilderness designation.

The eastern escarpment is steep red-brown andesite breccia, while the western side consists of gently sloping, black basalt flows. The area is dominated by typical Mojave Desert plants like barrel, cholla and prickly pear cactus, plus creosote bush and Joshua tree. At higher elevations are pinyon-juniper forests. This range also includes a large stand of teddy bear cholla, and black grama grass, both unusual for Nevada.

Both the El Dorado and Newberry moun-

Above: *Sunrise in the Amargosa Desert near Ash Meadows National Wildlife Refuge.*

Facing page: *Bristlecone pine and Mt. Charleston in the Mt. Charleston Wilderness, Spring Mountains, Toiyabe National Forest.*

Above: *Sandstone fins known as the Seven Sisters in Valley of Fire State Park, Muddy Mountains.*

Facing page, top: *Mount Charleston.* LARRY PROSOR PHOTO
Bottom: *Uptilted geological strata in the Muddy Mountains.*

tains border the Colorado River in Lake Mead National Recreation Area. Gold was discovered in the El Dorado Mountains as early as 1861, making it one of the first mining sites in the state. Both the Newberry and El Dorado mountains are composed primarily of Precambrian metamorphic rocks like granite and schists, with overlying outcrops of more recent volcanic basalts and tuffs. Neither range is very high, but the Newberry Mountains rise nearly 5,000 feet above the Colorado to 5,639-foot Spirit Mountain, the highest point in the range. Vegetation is typical of the Mojave Desert with black brush, yucca, creosote bush and cholla cactus. In addition, shrub oak grows in some of the canyons, and juniper is found at the highest elevations. Desert bighorn sheep, desert tortoise, and Gambel's quail inhabit the area.

Muddy Mountains

East of Las Vegas are the cliffs, deep canyons and peaks of the Muddy Mountains. A portion of this range is within Lake Mead NRA and Valley of Fire State Park, while the remainder is managed by the BLM and part of a 100,000-acre WSA. The area has many spectacular canyons and peaks for exploration; one, Anniversary Narrows, is only seven to fifteen feet wide, yet it is 400 feet deep!

The highly eroded and rugged fault block range is 23 miles long and reaches its apex at 5,432-foot Muddy Peak. The range is sedimentary in origin, originally deposited 200 to 300 million years ago in deep seas. Eons of shallow seas, and even deserts, followed, when sands that formed limestone piled high to create fossilized sand dunes. About 60 million years ago, the older, grayish limestone layers were uplifted by plate collision, and pushed eastward over the younger red Aztec sandstones today so visible in Valley of Fire State Park.

Mormon Mountains

North of Interstate 15 and the town of Moapa, and east of Highway 93, lie a group of mountains under BLM management—the Mormon, Meadow Valley, Delamar and Clover mountains. Most of them are roadless, forming a huge area of wild country directly east of the Desert Wildlife Refuge. The highest point in any of them is below 8,000 feet, but that doesn't mean there isn't some rugged country among their crags and canyons.

Farthest south, and about 75 miles northeast of Las Vegas, are the Mormon Mountains. Unlike many ranges in the Basin and Range province, the Mormon Mountains are more circular than linear, and approximately 18 miles across. The highest point, Mormon Peak, rises to 7,414 feet, for a total vertical re-

lief of more than 5,000 feet above Meadow Valley Wash to the west.

Like the Muddy and Spring mountains, the Mormon Mountains consist of older limestone formations overlying younger

sandstones. As in the other ranges, limestone dominates the peaks—which are extremely rugged, with deep, remote canyons, massive cliffs (some more than 800 feet high) and knife-edged ridges. Numerous caves are found in the central portion of the range and several possess stalactites, stalagmites and columnar formations.

Most of the range is covered by Mojave Desert vegetation like bursage, blackbrush, yucca and Joshua tree. Pinyon-juniper covers some of the higher peaks, along with a small relict stand of ponderosa pine near the top of Mormon Peak. Desert tortoise and desert bighorn sheep are both found in the range, as well as numerous pictograph and petroglyph sites. More than 162,000 roadless acres are under study by the BLM for potential wilderness designation.

Meadow Valley, Delamar mountains

Slightly north and west of the Mormon Mountains is the long, linear crest of the Meadow Valley Mountains—in places less

Like the Muddy and Spring mountains, the Mormon Mountains consist of older limestone formations overlying younger sandstones.

than a mile wide. The western slope is steep, while the eastern side is more gently sloped. Overall the range contains numerous jumbled, jagged peaks and hidden canyons, although the highest point is an unimpressive 5,700 feet in elevation. Most of the range is made up of sedimentary limestones and dolomites, some volcanic rocks, and quartzite, which is metamorphosed sandstone. Lower elevations are mostly desert shrublands, while limited amounts of pinyon-juniper cover the highest elevations. Desert bighorn sheep, desert tortoise and spotted bat are among the unusual species found here. Hackberry and Vigo canyons are popular hiking destinations. Some 186,000 roadless acres are contained within a BLM wilderness study area.

Northwest across the Kane Springs Valley from the Meadow Valley Mountains, and east of Highway 93, are the 50-mile-long Delamar Mountains, whose greatest elevation is atop 8,035-foot Chokecherry Mountain. These mountains are more mesa-like, dissected by ridges and canyons. One special feature of the range is one of the northernmost occurrences of the Joshua tree, which grows on the

slopes of the Delamars amidst sagebrush and juniper. A 126,000-acre WSA covers part of the range.

Along the eastern edge, gold and silver were discovered in 1889 and the town of Delamar sprang up. Water had to be hauled 12 miles from Meadow Valley Wash; hence, dry milling was the norm. This process produced a fine dust that caused the deaths of many residents, giving rise to the town's nickname: "widow maker." Nearly $15 million in gold was taken from the Delamar mines, making it the leading producer for the 1890s. Today Delamar is completely abandoned, although ruins are still standing.

Clover Mountains

Southeast of Caliente are the Clover Mountains. The roughly circular range is bounded on the south by the Tule Desert and on the west by Meadow Valley Wash, with its highest ridges rising to 7,400 feet. The range is composed limestone, quartzite, and brightly colored volcanic tuffs and other material from the Caliente caldera. Cottonwood Creek, which dissects the range on the southwest is a perennial stream, bounded by cottonwood, ponderosa pine, willow and ash. Elsewhere in the range are stands of Gambel's oak, plus aspen, although pinyon-juniper is the dominant forest cover. An 84,000-acre BLM wilderness study area centered on Cottonwood Creek, the major tributary draining the southwest corner of these mountains, covers part of the range.

Above: Sedimentary and igneous rocks in the Muddy
Mountains demonstrate the complex folding and thrusting
that created many of the mountains in southern Nevada.
Lake Mead National Recreation Area.

Facing page: Barrel cactus in the Desert National Wildlife
Refuge.

PROPOSED GREATER DESERT WILDLANDS ECOSYSTEM

Go a little north and east and cross paved Highway 95 and enter the 354,000-acre Spotted Range roadless area, mostly in the Desert WLR. Again, one dirt road separates this area from the 467,000-acre Desert-Pintwater Range, also in the Desert WLR. The 277,000-acre Hole in the Rock roadless area, split about equally between the wildlife refuge and BLM, lies immediately east, across another dirt road. Just south is the 468,000-acre Sheep Range roadless area, mostly in the wildlife refuge.

Then, crossing paved Highway 93, you almost immediately enter the 127,000-acre Delamar Mountains BLM roadless area, which is separated from the 186,000-acre Meadow Valley Mountains BLM roadless area by a road in Kane Spring Valley. Also east of Highway 93 and the Desert WLR is relatively small, 32,000-acre, Arrow Canyon roadless area. Finally, one more dirt road and railroad tracks in Meadow Valley Wash separate this area from the 163,000-acre Mormon Mountains BLM roadless area.

In total this is a minimum of 2,617,000 acres—one of the largest near-roadless land complexes in the lower 48 states, and virtually uninhabited.

At present the Greater Desert Wildlands Ecosystem is home to the largest concentration of desert bighorn sheep in the country, relict Pleistocene forests of white fir, ponderosa pine and bristlecone pine, plus dozens of other rare or endemic species from Palmer chipmunk, desert tortoise and kit fox, to endangered fish species like the Pahrump poolfish.

Although split into a number of units by a few dirt roads and one or two paved highways, the Desert Wildlife Refuge and adjacent Forest Service and Bureau of Land Management lands make up the largest nearly continuous roadless lands in Nevada, and one of the largest in the nation. Starting in the west and moving east, there is the 200,000-acre roadless area composed of both BLM and Forest Service lands centered on the Spring Mountains. Cross one dirt road and you enter the 180,000-acre Mount Stirling BLM roadless area, the northern extension of the Spring Mountains.

If all the qualified roadless public lands were eventually designated as wilderness, a few dirt roads were closed, the limited domestic livestock grazing terminated, and the area managed as a cohesive whole, this Greater Desert Wildlands Ecosystem would rival the Greater Yellowstone Ecosystem for biological, wilderness, recreational and aesthetic value, and could serve as both a scientific baseline and ecosystem reserve of international importance—all in the backyard of Nevada's largest urban area.

Above: *Yuccas at dawn in the La Madre Mountains, a subset of the Spring Mountains, northeast of Las Vegas.*

Facing page: *The Las Vegas Range in Desert Wildlife Refuge.*

INDEX

*Illustrations are indicated by **bold type***

Heli-skiing in the Ruby Mountains. LARRY PROSOR PHOTO